DELICIOUS MEMORIES

Stories and Recipes from a Czech-American Home

MARY STRETTON

Hearth PUBLISHING
HILLSBORO, KANSAS

Printed in the United States of America
by Multi Business Press, Hillsboro, Kansas

Publisher's Cataloging in Publication
(Prepared by Quality Books Inc.)

Stretton, Mary
Delicious memories: stories and recipes from a Czech-American home / Mary Stretton.
p. cm.
Includes table of contents.
Preassigned LCCN: 94-77377.
ISBN 1-882420-21-7
1. Stretton, Mary. 2. Cookery, Czech. Czech Americans—Wisconsin—Biography. I. Title.

TX723.5.C9S77 1994 641.5'9437'1'092
QBI94-1576

To Ella, my mother

ACKNOWLEDGEMENTS

Portions of "Tell Me About the Old Country" first appeared in *Viltis*, a Magazine of Folklore and Folk Dance, V. F. Beliajus, Publisher.

"Dish Nite at the Granada" first appeared in *The New York Antique Almanac*, The N.Y. Eye Publishing Company.

FOREWORD

Children have a great desire to be proud of their parents, but children of immigrants often find this desire difficult to achieve. Unfamiliar with a new country's customs, their parents will act awkwardly in certain situations, will attempt to deal with a challenging environment in inappropriate and sometimes embarrassing ways, will "talk funny." Their children feel a conflict: wishing to be loyal, yet wanting above all to assimilate, to become just like their American peers, and hoping that their parents, somehow, will do the same.

As the child of an immigrant mother, I was often aware of this conflict. But as I matured I began to realize that I had the advantage of choosing from the best of both worlds. Not only was I bilingual; I could also be bicultural. While my home was in the New World, my history was in the Old; and my mother's presence brought them together for me in many wonderful ways.

CONTENTS

The Consolation of Kolaches

Miss Martin introduced the new girl, Carolyn, to the class. We eyed and examined her with the straightforward curiosity of second graders.

"Carolyn is new in town and doesn't know her way back home yet," Miss Martin told us. "Is there someone who lives on Crawford Avenue near Hickory Street? Mary, don't you live over that way? Will you walk home with Carolyn this noon, and then come back with her after lunch?"

I nodded my head shyly, brushed back some wispy bangs, and took another look at Carolyn, who was being assigned a seat near the front of the room. A new girl to walk home with. A new girl with long brown braids and a freckled face. "I hope she's nice, and I hope she'll like me," I thought.

During the days that followed, I learned many things about Carolyn, who liked to talk. Her father was a school teacher who wanted to be a principal. He had a Master's degree. I didn't know what a Master's degree was, and I was ashamed to ask. One thing I knew for sure—*my* father didn't have one. He worked from seven until four in a factory and carried a lunchbucket.

Carolyn told me that her mother had been a teacher who was planning to join the Women's Club. She also informed me that her ancestors had come over on the Mayflower. Her mother, Carolyn said with a wide smile, had told her she should always be proud of that.

I knew about the Mayflower. The teachers talked about it on the day before Thanksgiving. Last November some of us had acted out the parts of Pilgrims in a class play, but I didn't feel very close to the Pilgrims. They wore plain brown clothes, always walked very solemnly to church, and never danced or sang.

Carolyn was curious about my mother. Mama often came to the door to say a few friendly words to her when she stopped for me on the way to school. "Your mother talks funny," Carolyn said. "She's got some kind of accent. Did she come from a foreign country?" I seemed to hear just a hint of pride, of superiority, in Carolyn's voice.

"What boat did your mother come over on?" Carolyn asked me. I didn't know the name of Mama's boat and asked her about it that evening. Mama told me she had come over on a ship called the Saxonia, which I thought was a funny-sounding name, not a pretty one like the Mayflower. Mama also told me that she had come over as a second-class passenger, something she seemed to think was important.

"If you come second class or first class, you don't go to Ellis Island. My cousin Joe didn't want me to go there, so he pay extra and I come second class. I am immigrant from Old Country who never saw Ellis Island!" she said with a little smile of self-satisfaction.

My friendship with Carolyn progressed. She lived only a block away, so I often visited her; I liked her piano and her black cocker spaniel. Carolyn's mother spoke as I was certain a former schoolteacher should speak, pronouncing her words very precisely. How wonderful it must be to have such a smart mother! A mother who could drive a car, who belonged to the Women's Club, who talked about directing children's plays at the Club in the coming spring...

Whenever Carolyn came to play in my house, I would take my mother aside and ask her to please stay in the kitchen. I didn't want Carolyn to listen to my mother's accent. I wished Mama could speak proper English all the time and would do more than just stay in the house all day, cleaning, washing, crocheting, embroidering, and baking Bohemian kolaches. I wished Mama would join the Women's Club.

I didn't realize that there were many things taken for granted in my life that other children would find fascinating, such as speaking in another language, receiving letters from a Grandma in Europe, and listening to my mother's stories about growing up in Bohemia. Speaking in Czech, Mama would tell me about how she helped her mother take care of her younger sister and three brothers. There were years of hardship during the First World War when her father was away serving as an artillery captain in the Bohemian army. The death of her older sister brought much grief. But then, with bewildered excitement, Mama found herself coming alone to a new country, working as a maid, learning a strange new language and customs.

I also took for granted the delightfully filling Bohemian foods—plump potato dumplings, noodle soup, liver dumpling soup, savory pickled sweet-sour red cabbage, mushrooms hand-picked in nearby woods, and Mama's ever-present raised dough kolaches, filled with prunes or poppyseed or sweetened cottage cheese or apricots. In addition there were the kolaches which looked like balls, called *buchty**, with the filling totally enclosed. My favorites were baked with sweet wine-purple grapes or the small purple plums that come in late summer. As a child I never regarded these foods as highly-desired but seldom-obtained treats; they were always available in their season. Instead, what I found delectable were foods that Mama seldom served, such as ham salad sandwiches, fried chicken, broiled steak, olives, and spaghetti.

Her pies were disasters because of their tough crusts. Mama was used to working with yeast doughs which can take a lot of handling, so she couldn't resist kneading her pie dough, which resulted in a hard crust. Pies are not an indigenous Czech pastry; Mama learned how to make them only after she came to this country, and somehow she could never learn to do the crusts properly. Once I tasted a lemon-meringue pie at Carolyn's house and was amazed at the flaky crust. I never would have admitted to her that my mother's pie crusts were tough and quite uneatable. In fact, whenever Mama would bring a pie to the table, my father would make his ritual joke about it, saying, "I'm going down to the basement to get my hatchet so we can chop the crust and cut up the pie. No knife'll do the job!"

Ours was a bilingual household—both languages coming easily and naturally, often spoken in combination, a funny mix of tongues. I was able to accept this way of speaking among other Czech-Americans, but as a small child I wanted my mother to speak English properly. An accent lowered her in my esteem—it was something to be hidden, kept quiet. Stay in the kitchen, Mama, when my friends come here to play. Especially when Carolyn comes....

A year passed. Then two years. Carolyn was an outgoing girl who made many friends. Sometimes I felt like a tag-along, standing in the schoolyard beside her, tracing designs with my shoe in the gravel, while she and her new friends gossiped and giggled. She seemed to have a lot in common with some of the well-to-do girls who lived in the Bay Shore area northeast of town, near the lake. She discovered Claire, a physician's daughter. Soon Carolyn ignored me for the most part at school and played with Claire at recess time. One day she told me she would be moving.

"Daddy's having a house built in Bay Shore. He's going to be the principal of North School. I'm going to live close to Claire and our

---

* The Czech *ch* is pronounced like *ch* in the Scottish "loch." "Kolach" is an Americanized spelling of the Czech word kolač, with the ch pronounced as in *watch*; i.e., "She watches her kolaches."

mothers are going to take turns driving us to school. It's nicer in Bay Shore because we can see the lake and there isn't so much traffic. We don't really like Crawford Avenue."

That evening I was irritable at supper and didn't want to eat. I went to my room and sat on my bed and cried for a while until Mama came to find out what was wrong. She carried a tray with Bohemian kolaches and a glass of milk.

"I bake nice apricot kolaches today," Mama said. "Maybe you like some with milk."

I did what came naturally to me when I was feeling sad—I asked Mama to sit on the bed and tell me a story.

"Mama, tell me about how you came over from the Old Country and the policemen met your train. Tell it in English."

I was going through a phase, still under Carolyn's influence, when I didn't want to be spoken to in Czech, which I felt was an unworthy language, spoken only by poor, ignorant immigrants.

Mama began the old familiar story in her rich Bohemian accent—the words stressed on the first syllable and rolling with strong no-nonsense *r*'s:

"It was beautiful spring morning when train pull into station. My cousin Joe, he was too busy with store to meet train, so he ask two policemen friends of his who can speak little Czech to meet me. So I was met at train and escorted to Cousin Joe's house by two policemen in police car!"

Mama laughed. Her warm, cozy voice cheered me, so I wiped my eyes and munched my kolach and listened with big eyes to the story I had heard so many times before.

Mama continued in a confidential tone: "You know, I bet people on train and in station think I was some kind of criminal!"

I started laughing too. Only Mama could be so funny. This could only have happened to her. It would never have happened to Carolyn's stuck-up mother. Come to think of it, I had never heard Carolyn's mother laugh.

Suddenly feeling better, I reached for another kolach.

"TELL ME ABOUT THE OLD COUNTRY"

I loved to listen to my mother's tales about her childhood in that far away land of Bohemia, which had not yet become part of the country of Czechoslovakia.* When my mother was young, Bohemia was still a part of Austria-Hungary, owing allegiance to the Emperor Franz Josef.

Mama, tell me about the time Grandma first saw Grandpa...

Mama came from a well-to-do family who lived in the small town of Holice, east of Prague. Her father was a bank treasurer; her mother, my lovely Grandma Růžena (translation: Rose), had been born in a large brick house which faced the town square of Polička, a city about forty miles from Holice. Mama enjoyed telling me the story, which her mother had told her, of Grandma Rose's first encounter with her husband-to-be.

Růžena and Otakar on their wedding day—late 1890's.

Rose, then a young woman of twenty-two, was standing by her upstairs bedroom window one morning, dreamily brushing her long dark hair, when she saw a handsome young man in a military uniform crossing the town square. Fair-haired, fair-mustached, his bearing erect and proud, he happened

* Czechoslovakia was created as a nation after the First World War. In 1993, it split into two separate countries: the Czech Republic and Slovakia.

to glance up as he strode along. He stopped abruptly and stared at a dark-haired vision, entrancing in a frilly white peignoir, standing in a second story window. The lovely vision looked down at him, gasped, blushed, and stepped back from the window. He came to himself and continued on his way. An excited Rose ran to her sister's room and cried dramatically, "Marie! I've just seen the man I'm going to marry!"

The young artillery officer, Otakar, made inquiries, and was told the young lady's name. He arranged to make her father's acquaintance, and at last met the girl who, as she had excitedly prophesied to her sister, became his wife about a year later.

Tell me about your family, Mama...

My mother was Rose and Otakar's second child; her sister Milada, called Míla, was barely a year and a half older. The two sisters were good friends and often inseparable. Míla was dark-haired like her mother; while Elinka, my mother, resembled Otakar with fair hair and blue-green eyes. A younger sister and two small brothers made a large, merry family in their roomy stucco home in Holice. Another boy was born soon after the First World War began.

Elinka as Little Lord Fauntleroy—1910

The young couple, Rose and Otakar, loved attending plays and acting in them. Early in their marriage they joined a drama group, often appearing in local productions of currently popular Czech plays as well as presentations of the classics and Czech versions of English and French dramas. Otakar, gradually growing portly from his wife's good cooking and his fondness for the excellent Bohemian beers, favored roles where he could strut about grandly, shouting orders—roles of kings, military heroes, or domineering heads of households. Rose, between pregnancies, took the parts of queens, noble ladies, or wronged and misunderstood wives.

Little Elinka enjoyed acting in plays as much as her parents. All their children had acting in their blood, but Elinka seemed to possess the greatest talent. "I memorized all parts, not just role I was playing," she often told me. "I had entire play memorized!"

Her favorite role, at the age of nine, was in the Czech version of "Little Lord Fauntleroy" in which she portrayed young Cedric Errol, the "little lord." It was a role which would later be made famous by Hollywood's popular child actor of the 30's, Freddie Bartholomew. Rose portrayed young Cedric's mother, and Otakar took the role of his grocer friend, Hobbs. The presentation of the play was so well-received that the cast took it on a short tour of some neighboring towns and villages.

This was perhaps the happiest time in the child Elinka's life—acting in a play with her parents, hearing the applause of an enthusiastic audience, realizing her talent and becoming aware of her potential.

"It was dream of mine at that young age to belong to *Národní Divadlo* (National Theatre) Company. People say to my mother she should send me to Prague to be actress, but she say no, my daughter belong here with her family. If she go to Prague, she will become spoiled from too much praise and attention. She will grow away from us and become like stranger."

Rose knew of the dangers and pitfalls awaiting naive girls from small towns who aspired to stage careers in Prague. Touring drama groups from larger cities occasionally presented plays in Holice, and their members were obliged to find lodgings with local families. A small room was made available in Rose and Otakar's home for an itinerant actress when needed. Rose listened to many a mournful tale from an aging, overly-rouged tragedienne who spoke of her dreary, impoverished existence after youthful dreams of success on the stage and an easy life upon retirement. This would not be her daughter's fate, Rose decided, and she remained firm in her resolve not to send Elinka into the allurements and perils of the life of a professional actress.

Mama, tell me about how you celebrated Christmas...

"First, we celebrated Feast of *Svatý Mikuláš*, St. Nicholas, on December 6. Three people would dress up as Saint, Devil, and Angel. There would be knocking on door. Three heavy knocks. Saint

Nicholas would come into house, followed by Devil and Angel. Saint would ask each child if he had been good and if he said his prayers every day. Children were scared. When they would answer their teeth would be chattering. Angel would write everything down that they said, and Devil would rattle his chain and make mean faces and growl. We were glad when they went away.

"Of course when we got older we knew it was only neighbors or relatives dressed up like this, but little children believe every bit of it!"

When I listened to my mother describe their home at Christmas time, I could imagine being there, seeing what she saw and doing what she did:

"My mother and maid decorated tree in parlor. This room was kept closed to children, who could not go in until Christmas Eve. We had real candles on tree, and we had to watch carefully so tree would not catch fire. My mother had many ornaments, very fancy, of glass. Other ornaments she made herself, from eggshells, or walnuts, or quills from chicken feathers. She would soften quills in hot water, then cut them into shapes like petals and form them into flowers with fine wires and decorate them with tiny beads. They were very delicate and pretty. Tree was so beautiful when all candles were lit. Every Christmas we each got one orange, which was big treat for us. We got many other presents, but only one orange!"

Otakar in right foreground, with white beard, serving as Captain in Bohemian Army, part of Austro-Hungarian forces—about 1916.

Oranges were imported and therefore very expensive. Even a family who was well off could afford only a few, usually at Christmastime.

"On Christmas Eve our supper was always fish, usually fried carp, or sometimes baked with prune sauce and served with special dumplings mixed with bread cubes. My mother made *Boži Milosti* at this time of year. They were small pieces of delicate dough, fried quickly like doughnuts and rolled in powdered sugar. We would gobble these up and ask for more, and there was never enough!

"After supper we would go to church, to Mass. Sometimes snow would be falling, everything so peaceful and white. Church was all lit up with candles, air filled with smell of incense, everyone was so happy, we were dressed in our best clothes, and my mother and father looked like king and queen..."

As she spoke a far-away look came to Mama's eyes. She was back in the Old Country, back in the days of her childhood when her world was serenely happy, surrounded by love.

Tell me about the war, Mama...

My grandfather was a commissioned captain of artillery in the Bohemian Army. When the First World War started, he was immediately called up to serve, leaving a pregnant Grandma Rose to cope with five children, aged five to fourteen.

There had always been servants to help, for they were a prosperous family. With Otakar's well-paying position as a bank treasurer, there had been no need to scrimp in their daily living. A maid would come every day, and other women came occasionally to do the heavy washing, ironing, and mending. Strong men also arrived as needed to wash walls, clean windows, or chop wood.

Rose did the cooking. Before her marriage, like most girls of good families at the time, she had been sent as a pupil to an esteemed hotel in Prague to learn the culinary secrets of the head chef of its restaurant. She returned home with her marriageability status highly enhanced, for now she was accomplished not only in the traditional Czech cuisine, but she could also prepare souffles, French sauces, roast beef rare with Yorkshire pudding, steak Tartare, Sacher torte, apple strudel and fruit puddings of various varieties and textures.

Grandma Rose learned her cooking lessons so well that when she married, her husband refused to eat any meals except those prepared by his wife. Although theirs was a household which could have afforded a cook in addition to their regular maid, he insisted no one could cook as well as his lovely Rose. Mama often enjoyed recalling how Grandpa would beam at Grandma with pleasure and anticipation when she set his favorite dishes before him. What a prize he had for a wife—what a cook! his twinkling eyes seemed to say.

With the war came the end of any extravagance; the soldier Otakar had to terminate his position with the bank and rely on the much lower pay, when it came at all, of an army captain. Extra household help could now seldom be afforded; the daily maid, called a *služka*, stayed on out of loyalty and moved in with the family, taking room and board in place of wages.

Those were difficult years for Rose, now forced to function as head of the household. She gave birth to her last child, a son. It had been a difficult birth and Rose's health had suffered. She worried constantly about her sickly youngster, fearing he would die. In years past, she had lost a baby in infancy and a tiny girl of almost three. She could nurse the baby only a short time; then she relied on Elinka to search out milk from farmers who were sometimes reluctant to part with their supply. Food was scarce during the war years. The army could commandeer provisions whenever needed, and grocery shelves were often bare of necessities for civilians.

Mila and Elinka—1912.

Elinka regularly walked from village to village carrying a pail or jug for the precious milk. An actress to the core, she could put on a piteous face for the farmer's wife and cry real tears as she told them of her mother's dilemma. Not above exaggerating even their truly urgent predicament, she would plead unabashedly:

"Please, *Paní Sedláková* (Mrs. Farmer), my baby brother is starving from lack of milk. He has gone two days now without food, his digestion is poor and he must have good fresh farm milk such as your lovely cows give. I have money to pay (here she would jingle her coin purse), no question of that, dear lady. If you would be so kind, please, spare us a few cupfuls for the baby… Ah, thank you, you are kindness itself, God will reward you!"

The farmer's wife, intrigued and moved by this lovely fair-haired girl, would pour out the milk as Elinka cried a few final thespian tears of gratitude.

Míla, the older sister, was never sent on these milk-gathering expeditions, for she did not possess Elinka's ability to throw herself into the role and ad-lib as necessary. Míla would have been embarrassed and was apt to end up in a seizure of giggling in spite of the actual seriousness of their situation. Realizing this, Rose gladly gave the role of milk-seeker to Elinka.

"I was ham actress, sometimes," Mama told me, "but I brought home lots of fresh milk for baby!"

With the end of the war came another burden for Elinka's family, one shared by families throughout the Continent and even the United States: the Spanish Flu. Míla, the plump and rosy-cheeked one, caught the dreaded illness. She recovered gradually, but in the aftermath of the Flu developed pneumonia. She fought the disease for several weeks, but her body was too weak to defeat this second infection. She died in a spasm of coughing, Elinka watching, horrified, as Míla fell back lifeless on her pillow.

"When people in town hear daughter from our family had died, everyone immediately think it was me," Mama said. "I was very pale, thin at this time, apt to get sick, always running out of church because I felt I was going to faint. Next Sunday, when they see me walk into church with my family, some women cross themselves and think it is miracle—I have come to life! Then when they find out it was Míla who died, they can't believe it. She always looked so strong, so healthy… Who can explain it?"

Although the war was over the family was in difficult circumstances. Otakar had returned from the battle fields a man prematurely aged, nearly broken by his experiences. His hair had turned white, his ambition and drive were shattered, and the death of his eldest daughter, so much the image of Rose in her youth, seemed a blow from which he could not recover. During the war another man had taken over his position in the bank, and Otakar had to find employment elsewhere. He became an insurance salesman, an occupation which paid only a fraction of his formerly large salary.

Rose worried constantly about expenses. She corresponded with an older sister who had emigrated to the United States with her large family several years before the war began. They were doing well in the new country, in the state of Wisconsin, and they were aware of Rose and Otakar's circumstances. Soon after the war ended, Rose's sister wrote to suggest that Míla, as the eldest daughter, join them in the United States. In later years it might be possible for some of the other children to follow. Rose's oldest nephew, already established as a grocer, sent the money for Míla's journey, but she had died a few days before the boat passage money arrived.

Now Rose turned to Elinka as the one who must play the role which had been denied her sister.

"At first I didn't want to go, I was afraid," Mama said. "At that time I wanted to be teacher. I had been good student, I liked to study. But there was no money for me to go on to school, to learn to be teacher. In America I would not know language, I could work only as seamstress or maid. But I wanted to help out family. I would be one less mouth to feed, and maybe I could send them money when I start to earn some. Maybe I could even send enough money so others in family could go to United States too. So I said yes, I would go."

And with many tears, with a reluctant parting from her family, at age nineteen Mama took her sister's place and began her journey to America.

Getting Acquainted in America

When my mother arrived in her new country, she came face-to-face with realities that she had not foreseen in her girlish anticipations. First there was the problem of language: if she wanted to work, she must have some knowledge of English. Her cousin Joe, who was a grocer, had become a U.S. citizen in 1914. He knew the importance of early and continued study of a new language. Immediately she was enrolled in "night school" where immigrants assembled one or two evenings a week to learn the language of their chosen land and to prepare themselves for citizenship.

"Sometimes I think I would never learn English," Mama told me. "It was such strange language, not like French or German which I studied in school. And it was nothing at all like Czech! And so many different kinds of people in class! They come from Italy, Poland, Germany, Denmark—everybody looking at everybody else, and who knows what they are thinking!"

Mama had plenty of opportunities to practice speaking English with her relatives, who were all eager to teach her American customs. Among the cousins were twin girls who were only a year younger, yet seeming to her so much older, wiser, and knowledgeable.

"I felt like such a 'greenhorn' beside them," Mama often told me. "That's what immigrants were called in those days—and I think my cousins laugh at me behind my back for my Old Country ways."

Mama attended movies with her cousins at every opportunity; even though the films were silent, she felt that the captions helped her grasp the language. Her love of acting, drama, and the stage drew her to the films. Later, for her relatives' amusement, she would imitate the dramatic poses, the rolling of wide eyes, and the nervous hand-fluttering of a Mary Pickford, Pola Negri, or Theda Bara.

Another step in the Americanization of Mama came with the cutting of her hair, which, as she often proudly recalled, was "long enough to sit on." Bobbed hair was now the style, and a much more practical style it was, especially for women who worked, whether in their homes, in offices, factories, or as domestic servants. They all welcomed the neatness and coolness of the new hairstyles and the feeling of freedom they gave.

"It was such relief to get rid of that heavy long braid!" Mama said. "My head felt so light, I thought it would fly off!"

For many years Mama kept her thick braid, a pale, golden brown shade, as a remembrance, wrapped in tissue paper and stored in a box. I recall her showing it to me when I was a child. I was happy to see that it was nearly the same color as my hair. Mother's hair darkened over the years, and by the time she was in her thirties it was a light brown shade, no longer golden.

After she learned a little English and was more at ease in her new environment, it was time for Mama to look for work. She was a skilled seamstress, having learned some of the trade at school and the rest at home from her mother. Most girls from the Old Country had learned to be "handy with the hands." They could crochet, knit, embroider, mend, and sew clothing. Mama always enjoyed sewing and had made almost her entire wardrobe before leaving Czechoslovakia. Now in her Wisconsin home she hoped to find work as a seamstress, but after much searching it seemed that there were no opportunities available. Setting herself up in her own business as a seamstress was at that time out of the question, for her knowledge of English was quite rudimentary and she was still learning American customs. Mama was eager to start work because she knew she must pay her cousin back the loan of money for her journey. She also hoped to save something from her earnings to pay for the passage of another family member.

It then came down to a choice between light factory-type work or employment as a domestic servant. Mama felt inclined toward the latter, feeling more capable in this kind of occupation. One of her cousins who worked in a factory helped Mama make a decision when she complained about the constant noise as well as the discomfort of having to sit down all day. "Go work as a maid," she told Mama. "Those rich houses have plenty of food, and you're undernourished anyway!"

In the long course of her employment as a live-in maid, Mama worked in several households. In some she remained only a few weeks, for the working conditions were extremely difficult, and domestic servants were treated with little consideration.

"In one house I was expected to sleep on cot in back hall, next to big ice box which drip, drip, drip all night. Lady of house wanted me to do all ironing, and she had it figured out how much time I should spend on each piece to iron. Shirt should take five minutes, fancy dress seven minutes, blouse three minutes, underwear two minutes—everything minutes, minutes!"

"Another lady wanted me to sew for her on my time off. She bring me all kinds of clothes to mend, patterns and fabrics for dresses to make for her, dresser scarves to embroider—and she give me no extra money for all this! I work there one month only! I was one greenhorn she wasn't going to take advantage of!"

Strict economy in the purchase of food was practiced in another household, even though the employer dealt in wholesale groceries. The lady of the house, when serving oranges for breakfast to her children, carefully cut each orange in half and gave a half to each child. No one would have dared to request a whole orange, and there was seldom a spare half for the maid. Cakes, too, were stringently portioned out: a dainty piece of a plain one-layer cake was served to each household member and an even daintier piece was left for the maid.

"One would think it was wartime and we were on rations," Mama said. "I work there for whole year, and believe me, I didn't gain one ounce!"

Another employer learned that Mama knew how to prepare noodles and dumplings, and she insisted that Mama prepare these in addition to her other duties as a maid. "This lady's husband want noodles or potato dumplings with nearly every meal," Mama said. "I was expected to be cook and maid and wash dishes for six people. Almost every night I cry into dishwater!"

Mama eventually found an employer who treated her well and didn't try to cheat or overwork her. She remained in this household for four years, learning to speak a better English under the coaching of this lady, who spoke graciously to her. She also took an interest in her family in Europe and made her feel at home. Years after Mama left this household, was married and had a child, this woman's husband, whose hobby was woodworking, made a small child's bench with handles for me. I loved my little bench, which was crafted of smooth mahagony, and as a child I would carry it with me from room to room. It remains one of my dearest possessions.

While attending night school Mama met other young immigrant

women who were employed as maids. Most of them made no denial that they had their eyes open to meet young men with good future prospects, and Mama listened to many a discussion as to the best places to make the acquaintance of future husbands.

"Go to dance on Saturday night at Polish Hall! That's the place!" she would hear her young friends say.

Her twin cousins scorned the Saturday evening dances. "That's no place to meet the better class young men! It's just the farmers and the factory fellows that go there!" they told her.

But Mama loved the polkas, the waltzes, and even the newer fox trots that were danced in Polish Hall. She and a friend or two would give the Hall a try one or two Saturdays a month. They would take a streetcar to the Hall and then return home in the streetcar's final run about midnight. It was only rarely that a girl would allow a young man she had met at the Hall to escort her home in his car. Who knows what he would try!

Mama was a good dancer, light on her feet, delicate, and pretty. She was seldom without a partner, and she made the acquaintance of several young men who had also come from Czechoslovakia or were of Czech descent. It was the custom for a man to walk up to a girl who looked promising and ask her if she wanted to dance. If she consented, the young man would introduce himself. The girl would then tell him her name, and they would glide off in a waltz or hop out in a polka.

At one time a temporary maid named Anka, an immigrant from Yugoslavia, came to work in the household where my mother was employed. She and Mama were able to communicate to a certain extent in their respective Slavic tongues. Because there were to be several guests staying for a month in this household, the new girl had been quickly hired. She had been in the States only a few months, but she was already proud of her ability to understand English. Anka resented any attempt on my mother's part to help in her duties or to translate something which she could not comprehend. Anka and Ella (as my mother was now called) had been given special permission for a Saturday evening off, for Anka was eager to attend a dance and Mama had volunteered to go with her.

Late that Saturday afternoon the lady of the house told Anka to fill the bathtub for one of her guests and to put a pair of silk pajamas and bathrobe in the bathroom. Anka dutifully filled the tub, then went to get the lady's pajamas and bathrobe. She passed Mama in the hall and said something in her native language. Mama wasn't sure, but it sounded as though Anka had said, "Americans are crazy. She wants me to put her robe in the bathtub! How silly!"

Mama stood in the hallway, watching, as Anka fetched the robe and pajamas and went into the bathroom.

"What are you watching me for, Ella? Go get ready for the dance!" Anka said to Mama in her Croatian tongue. Then she said in a contemptuous voice, "That woman wants her robe in the bathtub! Crazy Americans!"

Mama quickly said in Czech, "No, no, Anka! Don't put the robe in the tub!"

Looking at Mama with surprise, Anka insisted, "Yes! Yes! That's what she said, and I'm supposed to do what she said!"

Before Mama could stop her, Anka threw the lady's bathrobe into the water.

That evening Mama went alone to the dance at Polish Hall. Anka spent the time in her room crying, upset at the lady's reprimand and mad at Mama for not stopping her from doing what she thought she was supposed to do.

"Lady call her 'stupid greenhorn' and Anka get very angry," Mama said. "Anka should know better, but she was just girl from village. People from villages aren't very smart."

It seemed that Old Country town and city dwellers had always looked down on people from villages, considering them uneducated and doltish. "And no wonder," Mama said. "Most of them were farmers!"

She would soon change her mind about farmers. On that fateful evening of Anka's blunder, Mama met a man who had been born and raised on a farm and was destined to become her life partner.

"When I first dance with him, I never thought he would be one day my husband," Mama told me. "He was nice enough, polite, little shy. I had to make most of conversation. He was not flashy, full of smooth talk, like some 'sheik.' But I like his sincerity. I knew right away here was good, steady man. Man I could trust."

She trusted him enough that first evening to allow him to drive her home in his big, shiny, new Cleveland sedan which he had bought only a few weeks before. He was very proud of it and drove carefully and slowly, perhaps not so much to protect his car as to postpone saying goodnight to the girl with whom he had already fallen in love.

Ella and Rudy had a long courtship. She was in no hurry to

marry; there was still a large sum to pay off on her loan, and she was trying to send a small amount of money to Europe every month. Mama had been working for several years at a maid's salary of six or seven dollars a week, which didn't allow her to do much, if any, saving. She thriftily sewed most of her clothes and did without many of the luxuries that her friends and twin cousins could enjoy, such as fine chiffon scarves, beaded purses, silk stockings, jewelry, imported cosmetics and perfumes, and weekly appointments at a beauty parlor.

Letters from her mother in Europe were discouraging and at times made her weep in frustration: "My dearest Elinka, your father doesn't feel like working, he spends so much time drinking beer with his cronies...Zenda (her youngest brother) fell off his bicycle and hurt his foot and we had to take him to the doctor...Ota (her oldest brother) would like to get married and start a business but money is scarce—could you spare a little extra for him...Jara (the middle brother) is sick again, he is so thin...Your sister wants to become a nurse but there is no money for her school fees—dearest Elinka, could you spare some more money for her, so she can continue her studies..." Consequently the money she sent them from her meager earnings had to be spent on their immediate needs rather than being put aside, as she had hoped, to pay for another family member's journey to America.

Rudy took her to meet his parents, who were retired from their farm and lived in a small house in the city. She was happy to learn that they had come from an area of Bohemia close to her home town. She felt comfortable with these people and spent many an evening talking with them about the Old Country. They would call up nostalgic visions of a land that now existed for them only in their memories.

Mama's twin cousins were not thrilled about her future when she told them she planned to marry a farmer who now worked in a factory.

"When I get married I'm going to make sure that it's to a professional man," one of them told her. "I'll just bide my time and wait, and one day he'll come along." (Unfortunately he never did, for this lady died unmarried in her seventies.)

The other twin was a bit more sympathetic to Mama and told her she was sure that getting married, even to a man who had been a farmer, was better than working as a maid, serving other families.

Mama always laughed whenever she told me about her twin cousins' reactions. "When they find out my farmer had some money in the bank, then they think maybe I made good choice after all!"

Rudy wanted to help Ella and urged her to accept money from him so she could pay off her loan. But Ella, being proud and stubborn, refused to marry him until the loan had been paid off with her own earnings.

And when it was finally paid, Mama accepted an engagement ring and notified her employers that she was going to be married. It was time, she told them happily, to live her own life and be the mistress of her own household.

Rudy and his new Cleveland—1926.

Ella & Rudy by Lake Michigan—late 1920's

Travels with the Cleveland

My father owned a slate blue 1926 Cleveland sedan which he kept in good running condition until way into the 40's. He spent nearly as much time repairing that durable car as driving it. Some of my earliest memories are of him emerging headfirst, grease-grimed and sweating, from underneath that big, box-like automobile.

Newer and sleeker cars came and went over the years to take up residence in our double garage, while alongside them the old Cleveland clung to life, nursed along by my father and uncle. Living with his family just down the block, Uncle Oscar was always available to lend a hand or screwdriver or wrench or maybe just advice when some sort of major surgery was required.

"How's she doing?" Uncle Oscar would ask eagerly, squatting beside my dad who was stretched under the car with only his legs visible. He pounded, thumped, turned screws, squirted oil and, more often than not, cussed at the ornery vehicle.

"She needs new points, I guess," my dad might say, or "Let's try her out—I think she'll be okay now."

If I saw my father get into the car I would let out a howl, hop onto the wide running board and beg to be taken along. I loved to ride in the Cleveland and never wanted to miss an opportunity to do so.

Some of my happiest summer afternoons came when my dad allowed me to accompany him on a fishing trip after work. He and my uncle were employed in a factory near the Lake Michigan shore, and when the fish were biting, word would spread quickly that "They're hitting off the south pier!" As soon as the whistle blew, all fishing enthusiasts would rush home, eager to snatch up their gear for an assault on the fishermen's pier.

I'm sure my father would have preferred only the company of his brother, for I was bound to be a nuisance and squeamishly refused to bait my own hook. But my joyful enthusiasm would strike a responsive chord in him, and no doubt remembering his own happy youthful fishing expeditions, he would consent.

Then I would run eagerly for my jacket and rubber overshoes, while my dad loaded the Cleveland with fishing paraphernalia: buckets, bait, string, bamboo poles, a tiny box in which he kept his hooks (imbedded in corks), sinkers, bobbers, and all the humble little necessities of the fisherman's craft. Bouncing with anticipation, I would sit on the worn gray mohair of the back seat, my hand clutching my short pole, as my father maneuvered the car to the lakeshore, only a few miles away, and talked with Uncle Oscar about the prospects for the day's catch of perch.

Going twenty miles per hour in the Cleveland, as it rattled, shook, and shuddered, I had the sensation that we must be going fifty at least. It was fun, exhilarating, and even a bit dangerous, I thought, to be a passenger in such a dashing old car. Suppose something fell off—suppose a wheel came loose, a door dropped off, or we left the rear bumper behind somewhere? When my dad pressed the button in the center of the steering wheel, the horn sounded a hoarse "Ah-OO-dah! Ah-OO-dah!"—a far more classy sound than the silly *toot, toot,* of the other cars.

Certain summer afternoons were devoted to minnow-catching, when my dad, Uncle Oscar, and I would embark on a longer journey in the Cleveland. Our destination would be a strip of beach north of the city—land owned by my father and his six brothers, a part of the inheritance left them by their immigrant father who had homesteaded a farm on that southeastern Wisconsin lakeshore.

Bumping along the dusty dirt roads, we would pass the familiar farms of my father's boyhood. The mailboxes, sitting on wooden posts, bore the names of Czech settlers who had peopled the area a few generations ago: Vorlicek, Jenista, Hrouda, Smercek.

"Novak's potato plants look good," my dad would comment.

"Those cabbages of Petura's over there," Uncle Oscar would point out, "don't look so great. Need some rain."

They discussed the neatness of this farmyard, the rundown look of that barn; they speculated about a predicted drought; they wondered if the Dvoraks still had those excellent Muscovy ducks for sale. Listening to their talk, I had a sense of belonging to this farming land, a realization that my roots were intermingled with those of all who lived in the area. Our Bohemian forefathers had migrated from a landlocked country; they settled in this new nation near the shores of a large inland lake more like a sea, and they prospered in the good rich soil. Over the years these farmers had learned to respect the quick-changing moods of the lake. They seldom rowed very far offshore in their small wooden rowboats, which were used occasionally for short fishing expeditions.

On minnow-catching afternoons my dad and uncle wore bathing suits under their shirts and trousers. Once at the beach, they would remove their outer clothing and wade into the chilly water, pulling a wide, finely-woven fishermen's net between them. If lucky, they would scoop in a large amount of tiny minnows, ideal as bait for the larger perch. The minnows would be kept in buckets of water until the next day's fishing trip.

I was not allowed to venture far out in the water, for the undercurrent was strong there and Dad was careful to heed my mother's warnings not to let me take any chances. I spent my time picking up tiny shells from the sand, watching the changing colors of the water, and running barefoot along the beach. I reveled in the blue sky, the shush-shing of the surf, the mewing of the gulls, and the knowledge that this was our own, our very own beachland to enjoy as we pleased.

On the way home, to reward themselves for a good catch of minnows, my dad and uncle would stop for a beer at the Five Mile Road tavern. I stayed inside the Cleveland because I disliked the sour tavern smell of beer and pretzels. Dad always brought me a glass of my favorite grape soda with slivers of ice. I would sip my drink lazily, contentedly going over the afternoon in my mind and thinking about the fishing day to come. I would anticipate the good supper Mama would have waiting for us, beginning with one of her many flavorful soups such as cauliflower, lentil, or even beer soup. Next would come sweet-sour cabbage and sausages, or roast pork with dumplings, or that tender marinated beef dish called *svíčková*. Later, for dessert, she might serve a treat like cherry *bublanina*, fruity, sweet, and crusty. Leaning back, savoring the bubbly soda and my dreams, I felt warm, happy, safe in the old Cleveland.

I knew that if I asked him very nicely, and hadn't spilled any soda on the mohair seat, my dad would drive the long way home, past the lighthouse and the golf course. This would give me a few extra minutes to pretend I was the only airplane passenger on the dangerous lakeshore run, with my father and uncle as the brave pilot and copilot who were flying us safely home.

MAMA AND THE RICHBUCKS

The hand-lettered invitation was on pale pink paper with a flowered border. "COME TO BETTY LOU'S PARTY!" it read. "BETTY LOU'S MOMMY AND DADDY WILL TAKE YOU FROM SCHOOL TO BETTY LOU'S HOUSE, AND WHEN THE PARTY IS OVER WE'LL DRIVE YOU HOME! ISN'T THAT NICE?"

Yes, it was very nice, and like any third-grader, I was thrilled and couldn't wait for the day of the party. Finally the great day came, but at school that afternoon I started to get the feeling that something was wrong. Something that involved the party and me.

It couldn't have been my clothes.... I was dressed nicely enough in ruffled pink organdy, my favorite party dress that I had already worn to two cousins' wedding receptions. My brown oxfords were almost new, highly polished, and quite presentable-looking. However, I wished my mother had let me wear my Sunday-best patent leather Mary Janes like the other invited girls. But it was a cold November day, and the sky had looked like snow was coming, so "You must wear brown tie shoes today," my mother had decreed.

No, it wasn't my dress or my shoes. Something else was wrong. Something, I finally realized, was missing. I hadn't brought a big paper bag to school with me that afternoon. Carolyn had brought one and so had Janet, Audrey, Phyllis and the other invited girls. They had all brought mysterious, rustling brown paper bags and were acting silly and secretive, trying to hide the bags in the shelves under their desk tops.

Then Carolyn smirked at me in that superior way of hers and opened her crinkled brown bag just a bit to let me peek inside. I saw something glistening, all pale green and silky.

"Isn't that a beautiful ribbon?" Carolyn whispered behind her hand, so crabby old Miss Davidson wouldn't hear. "My mother bought it special. Promise you won't tell Betty Lou... I'm giving her a dresser set!"

It was only then that I understood I had been invited to a birthday party, only I hadn't known it was Betty Lou's birthday, and my mother in her Old Country innocence hadn't guessed that it was to be a birthday party. The invitation, after all, hadn't even mentioned a birthday.

What could I do? Would I dare go to Betty Lou MacFarland's party without a present for her? What would I say to Betty Lou? I didn't really know her very well; she sat on the opposite side of the room and played with girls I barely knew. Should I pretend to be sick and go home? I already felt a little sick. But to miss out on a party...this was too much to ask of an eight-year-old girl.

I went. Betty Lou's mother drove five of us in a big blue car, followed by her father with another bunch in a big black car. Two cars for one family! Betty Lou must be rich! We were driven to a large, two-story red brick house on North Lake Drive, a boulevard in a fancy section of our city near the lake, where, as my father often pointed out, the "richbucks" lived. So Betty Lou and her parents were richbucks.

A wide staircase led up to the second floor, where Mrs. MacFarland took our coats and laid them on a lavender silk bedspread. Betty Lou had a soft white rug in her room, an ample, sink-down-into rug, not like the lumpy little rag rugs my mother would crochet. The fluffy curtains were pale yellow with deep ruffles, and her bedroom had two windows that looked down into a garden.

This wonderful house left me speechless and dazed. Downstairs there was a fireplace with a snapping fire throwing off heat and orange sparks. The long table was set with gleaming dishes on white linen. There was even a maid to serve the food. It was the first time I had ever tasted fruit cocktail in red gelatin topped with whipped cream. Birthday cakes with candles were a familiar sight (Mother baked one for me every year), but fruit in red gelatin with whipped cream! It was almost too much to bear.

Then came the time for opening presents. In my excitement at all the wonders of Betty Lou's house, I had forgotten about my missing gift. Maybe they wouldn't notice....

Betty Lou's mother was the model of good manners and tact, but my so-called best friend, Carolyn, wasn't. After all the presents had been opened and admired, Carolyn blurted out, "Mary didn't bring any gift. Where's your present for Betty Lou, Mary?"

I wanted to die. I hated Carolyn and could have shoved her into the fireplace. Betty Lou's mother, pretending she hadn't heard, started pushing furniture around for a game of "musical chairs," but Carolyn's voice rose higher, demanding attention. "Mary didn't bring Betty Lou a present, Mrs. MacFarland!"

I don't know what got into me, but I looked the woman straight in the eyes and said, "My present isn't ready yet. I'll bring it to school tomorrow."

"Why, of course, dear, but you didn't have to bring a present," Mrs. MacFarland said soothingly. "Betty Lou doesn't expect a present from everyone."

But Betty Lou did. I saw the look she gave her mother.

You'll get your present, I thought. But what would it be? We were still in the Depression, and my dad had just recently returned to work after being on strike for several weeks. Gifts cost money, and even at my young age I knew that money was often scarce in our household. I had been begging for a canary in a green cage for a year, but my dad kept telling me that he just couldn't afford it.

When I came home early that evening, full of ham salad sandwiches, fruit cocktail, gelatin, whipped cream, and birthday cake, my mother asked me, "Well, how was party?"

When Mama spoke English, she seldom used the words *a*, *an*, or *the*, for Czech has no *a*'s, *an*'s, or *the*'s as parts of speech. In Czech, when you say, "I have coat," your meaning is clear, and you don't need an *a* or a *the*. My mother had long ago stopped trying to learn when to use *a*, *an*, or *the* because she could never get it right. It was hard for her to figure out where to put the accent in English words, so she solved that problem by always putting it on the first syllable, which is what one does most of the time when speaking Czech.

"Well, how was party?"

"Mama, it was a *birthday* party!"

"*Birthday* party! Why didn't they say so in invitation?"

"I don't know. Maybe they forgot. But I have to bring a present. All the other girls brought her a present and I was the only one who didn't."

"Then you must give her present. What kind of present you think she likes?"

"Oh, I don't know, Mama! Something nice."

I thought about the gifts Betty Lou had received. A dresser set from Carolyn, a jewelry box from Janet, a stuffed pink kitten, a box of handkerchiefs, a set of paints, a necklace, a game of Chinese Checkers... What could I give her? What could we afford?

"Mama, I told her mother I'd bring the present tomorrow because it wasn't ready yet."

"Wasn't ready yet? What are you going to give her?" Mama gave a little laugh. "Kolaches I baked today?"

My mother baked Bohemian kolaches two or three times a week. Kolaches are a type of pastry made from sweet raised dough, with fillings of prunes, or apricots, or sweetened cottage cheese, or poppyseed (mixed in a special secret way known only to Czech cooks, who bequeath kolach recipes to their daughters as the richest of heritages). Kolaches are homey, nourishing, and delicious. They were as much a part of my childhood as apples, milk, and bologna sandwiches.

"Oh Mama, no! I can't give something like *kolaches* to Betty Lou! It has to be something like hankies or a bracelet...something pretty. Betty Lou's folks are richbucks."

"So! Richbucks! Well, we see."

Mama went into the living room to talk to my dad, who was reading the newspaper. My dad worked hard as a laborer in a factory. He carried a lunchbucket and started work at seven. I can still remember how my mother would brew coffee in the morning for his thermos. She would mix the coffee with milk and sugar in a large white pitcher with a chipped top, and if any was left over after she had poured it into the thermos, she would give me a taste. It was the best coffee in the world.

I could hear the murmur of their voices while I waited in the kitchen. My mother had told me long ago never to "mix in" when she was talking to my dad, especially if these conversations concerned finances and our lack of them. Money was always needed for an unexpected something at school, for some new clothes, to buy a special item for the house, or for cooking. My father's desire was to save as much of it as possible in order to "bank something" in his meager savings account. He would grumble sometimes and complain; she would whisper and plead.

When she returned to the kitchen, Mama looked disappointed and a little worried.

"Daddy says he got nothing to spend for present," she told me. "Maybe I make something for your Betty Lou Richbucks."

"Mama! Her name isn't Richbucks!"

"All right, all right. I know. Let me think." She murmured something in Czech. Although I could speak Czech, having learned it before I learned English, I was ashamed to admit this to my girlfriends. I felt somehow that Czech was a totally unrefined language, inferior to English, and therefore not to be acknowledged as my cradle tongue.

"*Co budeme dělat když nemáme peníze*?"*

"Mama! Please speak English!"

"All right. I think I got idea."

Mama went upstairs to the attic. I could hear her rummaging around, opening and closing storage cabinets and the lid of her precious old trunk which she had brought with her from the Old Country when she was only nineteen.

When Mama came back she was smiling. She was carrying something wrapped in yellowed tissue paper.

"Look, Mary, what I found!"

She unwrapped the tissue and showed me a pretty little pink and white crocheted basket, about four inches high, which she said was stiffened with sugar-water. The basket held a dozen tiny, delicate crocheted flowers of all colors. The green leaves were also crocheted, and the stems were fine wires wrapped with narrow strips of dark green cloth. It was a delectable little treasure of a bouquet in a basket—ideal for a young girl's dresser top.

But it would never be right as a gift, for it was old, the colors were fading, and here and there the crochet thread was frayed or torn.

Mama saw my dismayed face and said quickly, "I make new one. Tonight. I got plenty crochet thread, and I can follow pattern from this one. Tomorrow you have nice present for Betty Lou."

Mama must have stayed up until the early hours that night, crocheting steadily and swiftly, sure of herself and her art. She had told me once that she had learned to crochet soon after learning to read. Watching the thread form into intricate designs of stitches and loops while her slender steel crochet hook flicked quickly in, out, and around, I could easily believe that she had almost been born with a crochet hook in her hand. No one could crochet as neatly and as fast as Mama.

The next morning the basket and flowers were ready. Mama had soaked the pale pink basket in sugar-water, shaped it around a small glass, and let it dry overnight in the oven which she had warmed up just enough. In the morning she took the basket out of the oven and slipped it off the glass. It stood up stiffly by itself, making a holder for the crocheted flowers that she carefully arranged inside.

"Oh, Mama…it's beautiful! How can we wrap it so it won't get bent?"

---

* "What are we going to do if we don't have the money?"

Mama had thought of that too. She had pasted shelf paper over an old cylinder-shaped oatmeal carton and lined it with tissue paper. She lowered the flower basket into the carton and gently put on the cover. A perfect fit. Then she showed me some sky blue wrapping paper which she had been hoarding in a drawer, as well as a white silk ribbon she had ironed until it looked like new. A few snips of her scissors, a little folding and tucking of paper, some tidy ribbon-fastening—and there was my present for Betty Lou, as nicely wrapped as any she had received at her party.

"There! You give this to Betty Lou today, and say you are sorry it is late. And..." Mama looked a little self-conscious as she handed me a flat box neatly wrapped in white shelf paper. "You say to Betty Lou this is for her mother. Something extra from me because they have to wait for present."

I didn't have to ask Mama what the flat box contained. Kolaches. Mama's eternal gift of friendship. Ever since I could remember, Mama had been baking kolaches and giving them away. To Mrs. Barta, whose feet were bothering her and who couldn't do her own baking. To Mrs. Baker, across the street, who was getting too feeble to bake. To old Mr. Callawert, the widower down the block, who let me play with his cat. To our many relatives who were forever dropping in for visits. To anyone that Mama thought would enjoy some good homemade bakery. She would give as easily as she would breathe.

That morning I set off for school feeling happy and relieved. I was carrying a big, brown, crinkled paper bag into which Mama had put the two gift boxes. Betty Lou would get her present, and I just knew she would like it as well as any she had received at her party.

Although I felt embarrassed about the kolaches, at age eight I was too young to rebel and refuse to take them. Mama probably knew best, but I had some doubts about whether Mrs. MacFarland would find these simple Bohemian pastries a proper addition to their more elegant diet. If only I could trade them for some more of that fruit gelatin and whipped cream!

When Carolyn saw my brown paper bag at school that morning, she looked surprised. "If you brought a present for Betty Lou, you're too late," she said. "Her birthday is over and done with!" She stuck out her tongue at me, but old Miss Davidson saw her and told her she would have to stay after school for making faces.

As for Betty Lou, she acted as though it was never too late for a birthday present. "Oh, thank you, Mary, thank you!" she said happily, as I gave her the gift box during recess time. She quickly tore off the wrapping paper and ooh'd and aah'd over her gift while a small crowd of girls collected around us.

"It's the best present of all!" she declared, holding the basket up by its stiff handle for all the admiring girls to see. Carolyn looked disappointed, but she didn't dare make any more faces because Miss Davidson was watching.

Betty Lou said she would give the other box to her mother as I had requested. "Is it a secret?" she asked.

"Sort of," I said. "Just something from my mother to yours." Wild animals tearing me apart wouldn't have made me tell her that my mother had sent along a batch of plain old Bohemian kolaches.

A few days later, as I was starting to walk home from school with Carolyn, someone waved to me from a big blue car sitting at the curb. It was Betty Lou's mother.

"Yoo-hoo, Mary," she called. She was waving a white envelope. "Here, give this to your mother, dear," she said. "I wanted to call her, but...I guess you don't have a phone, do you?"

"No, we don't," I said, taking the envelope, wondering what could be inside. It gave off a faint scent of perfume.

Mrs. MacFarland waved goodbye as I walked away with Carolyn. Whenever Carolyn was in a generous mood she would favor me with the pleasure of her company during the walk to or from school. She called herself my "best friend" in a way intended to make me feel as though she were doing me a great honor. She eyed the envelope with curiosity.

"Why don't you have a phone?" she asked. "We've always had a phone. Doesn't your mother ever want to call her friends?"

"She goes over to Mrs. Baker's house when she wants to call somebody," I said. "And when anybody wants to call us, they call the Baker's house."

We had many relatives who often came to visit us, but they had no telephones. There were plenty of family get-togethers without phoned invitations; dropping in on friends and relatives without prior notice was the accepted way of doing things among us. I had never felt deprived because of not having a telephone.

I gave Mama the envelope when I got home, and she looked at it with surprise.

"Letter for me from Mrs. MacFarland? What she want? I hope

nothing wrong with kolaches!"

Mama opened the letter carefully. She read it slowly, then she read it again. A slow smile warmed her face.

"Guess what, Mary! Your Betty Lou's mother—she wants me to bake more kolaches!"

Mrs. MacFarland had been so impressed with Mama's "delightful exotic pastries" that she wanted to serve them at a meeting of a ladies' bridge club she had just joined. In her letter she asked my mother if she would be willing to bake some the following week, and she offered to pay my mother whatever she asked.

"Well, what you think? Should I bake some kolaches for Betty Lou's mother?"

I didn't know what to think. My mother baking for somebody and getting paid for it? It was almost as if she were going to work outside the home. No married lady of my acquaintance did anything like that. Married women tended the house and raised their children. When their husbands came home from work, the men would make jokes about the easy life a woman had, listening to programs like "Pepper Young's Family" or "Our Gal Sunday" on the radio. It was true that Mama had her favorite soap operas, which she would listen to faithfully; but while she listened she would sew, crochet, dust furniture, or mix up a new batch of kolach dough. Her hands were never idle.

"I think it's good idea," Mama answered her own question. "I bake nice kolaches, charge little bit, and maybe make little money."

Mama carefully composed a letter: "Dear Mrs. MacFarland, I bake you nice kolaches like you ask. What you like? Apricot, prune, poppyseed, cottage cheese? You let me know?"

I took the letter to school and gave it to Betty Lou, who brought an envelope with her mother's reply the following day. After a few more letter exchanges and a message or two over the Bakers' telephone, Mama finally had her first order for kolaches clear in her mind. The next week she did her shopping for poppyseed and dried apricots.

My dad objected to the high grocery bill and grumbled more than ever.

"Don't worry," Mama reassured him. "You get it all back, and extra besides."

And she was right. After Mrs. MacFarland's club meeting, Mama started receiving other requests for kolaches. Perhaps Mrs. MacFarland, who had driven over to our house to pick up her order, realized we could use some extra money and had dropped a few hints to her friends. Or maybe some of the bridge club ladies had found the kolaches so delicious and unusual they just had to have more to serve family and guests. However it happened, kolaches seemed to become the "in" thing to serve at certain club meetings or parties. Mama, evidently, became known as the sole source of supply. There were Bohemian bakeries in town which sold kolaches, but Mrs. MacFarland's friends seemed to be unaware of their existence.

Her kolaches weren't the only thing that became famous. Mama began to get orders for crocheted baskets and flowers, and she sat up many a night with her crochet hook flicking away at high speed.

It didn't take long before Mama had almost more orders than she could handle. Old Mr. Baker started complaining to my Dad about his feet getting tired from all the running he was doing, across the street from his house to ours, to summon Mama to the telephone. Mama decided the time had come to do something drastic.

"We need phone," she said to my dad.

"Who pays for it?" my dad asked.

"I pay for it. From kolach money and flower basket money. Those richbucks, they like my baking and my crocheting. They pay me enough so I get profit. With profit I pay for phone."

We were soon the envy of our relatives with our shiny black telephone, but my dad warned my mother never to reveal to them who was paying for our phone bill. A man, after all, was supposed to be the sole supporter of his family.

Mama told me privately that she had no intention of remaining in the "kolach business." "It takes too much time. I rather spend my time for my own family. If your Daddy was gone, if I was widow, it would be different thing. But this is just for earning little extra. I think maybe soon Daddy get raise, and then he can pay for telephone."

When the United States entered the Second World War, my father started working many long hours overtime. His factory shifted from making small jacks for cars to producing large lifts for army trucks and airplanes; many a time our telephone summoned him to work Saturdays or even Sundays to help get out a military rush order. He was able to "bank something" every week; his savings account grew and he bought a war bond every month. He no longer grumbled about money; now he complained about his aching back, the Nazis, and gasoline rationing.

Mama called all her customers and told them she would be taking no more orders for kolaches or flower baskets. "Until duration," she said, but I knew that Mama never really intended to resume full-scale production again.

I knew Mama worried about her family in Czechoslovakia. She had heard from them occasionally during the German occupation, but the letters were always censored, so she knew her relatives were being careful not to reveal the full story of their hardships. After the United States entered the war, there was of course no mail exchange, and Mama had no news from her family at all. It was the waiting, she told me, that was the hardest.

She wanted to do something to help our soldiers in a more personal way, so she turned some of her energy to knitting woolen squares, six inches by six inches, for the Red Cross. The knitted squares were collected and sewn together into afghans which were sent to convalescent hospitals for wounded soldiers. Mama always managed to knit a small delicate design, a flower or a bird, in a contrasting color, into the center of each of her squares. It would make the afghan look more lively, she said, and "maybe help cheer soldiers up."

As soon as the war in Europe ended, Mama received a telegram from her family. All were safe and well, the message in garbled English said, except for her brother Jara, who had died of complications from surgery for a septic appendix. Grief and joy were mixed in Mama's heart. She mourned alone, letting me see only her happiness that the remaining members of her family—mother, sister, youngest brother, nieces and nephews—were well. She busied herself with sending them packages of food and clothing; hardly a month went by without Mama preparing a large parcel for her overseas relatives.

One day I came home from school and found a yellow canary in a green cage warbling away in our living room. I was delighted not only to have the pet I had wanted for so long, but to know that we could now afford to buy a few luxuries. At that time I thought my dad had paid for the canary; but now when I remember my mother's beaming face, I realize that she had spent the last of her richbuck money to make me happy.

Cemetery Road

Old Mrs. Blaha was the unofficial mourner at the Czech funerals. Because her two sons ran the Five Mile Road Tavern, she knew all the Czech farming families in the surrounding area as well as many of their city relatives, and she took an active interest in their lives.

The Five Mile Road Tavern was on the way to the cemetery, so my father and uncle often stopped there for liquid refreshment after a session of watering or planting flowers on Grandma and Grandpa's graves. Mrs. Blaha would treat them to the latest news and gossip concerning the Pishnys, the Holubas, the Janeckys, the Polivkas, or the Makovskys. They would take in this entertaining information as gladly as their beers.

Flower-planting sessions occurred around the latter part of May, several days before Memorial Day, or as we called it then, Decoration Day. Although there were five more brothers in my father's family, for some unknown or forgotten reason my dad and Uncle Oscar had been chosen for the honor of buying and planting the cemetery flowers, which were traditionally petunias of many colors. This custom had been followed for many years, and as a child I always looked forward to the ride among the May blossoms and scents down what I privately had named "Cemetery Road."

It was a peaceful and quiet road, gently undulating through farming country: a byway lined with graceful elm, hickory, walnut, beech, and crabapple trees. As the years went by it became my familiar and special back road, turning west off the highway for a few tranquil miles until the iron fence bordering the cemetery was reached.

A mourning dove was always cooing off somewhere in one of the cemetery's pines, its muted, plaintive call seeming to match the sadness in a soul downhearted after a visit to the grave of a loved one. In my childhood I came to associate mourning doves with cemeteries and thought that was were they lived and belonged. Later I was amazed to discover that they could also live in cities and would sing their soft *coo-ah, coo, coo* undisturbed by morning traffic.

Although I was an only child, I was fortunate to have a large extended family of uncles, aunts, and cousins on both my father's and mother's sides. There were many family get-togethers, picnics, showers, weddings, reunions, and inevitably, a funeral, either of a family member or a friend of the family. At every Czech funeral of my childhood that I can remember, Mrs. Blaha was present. And she always made her presence known by her unmistakable vocalizations.

"Oh, Mrs. Cernohorsky, what will you do without your Anton?" Mrs. Blaha would put her arms around a sad-faced widow and begin to sob. "How you will miss him! Just like I still miss my poor Josef! Oh, Josefku, why did you leave me alone so soon? Ten years a widow I am already! Oh, you will miss him! You will be lost!"

The unfortunate widow, stoically bearing up until then, was undone, and would begin weeping inconsolably. At this, Mrs. Blaha, having done her best, tried to lessen the damage by an attempt at consolation.

"Don't cry, Mrs. Cernohorsky, at least his troubles are over. Yours are just beginning, but you are strong, you can bear it, God will give you strength. Here, lean on me, cry all you want, ten years and I am still crying, wait and see, it's not all that bad, someone always takes care of a poor widow. We don't know how much we can miss them until they are gone, and they go too soon… Oh, oh…how terrible, your poor Anton, he went too soon…."

Moaning and wailing, Mrs. Blaha would be led away from the disconsolate widow, the unhappy recipient of her incomparable sympathy.

And so it went at every funeral. Occasionally there would be talk of barring Mrs. Blaha from the funeral service, but this was always vetoed as being too cruel a punishment for the poor woman whose only intent was to aid and comfort the bereaved.

Mama felt Mrs. Blaha was only indulging herself. "It makes her feel good to cry and get all her pain off her chest," Mama would say. "She doesn't realize she make other people feel worse by how she carry on. She should know better and restrain herself."

Often the funeral home was crowded on the evening before the funeral with the same people who would be present the following day. Acquaintances were renewed, nostalgic memories were called forth, old friends greeted each other with tears in their eyes, and lengthy conversations took place regarding the merits of the deceased. What started out as a solemn night gathering with hushed voices gradually began to lose its solemnity. The hum of voices grew louder, and smiles began to replace quivering lower lips. Soon a relaxed atmosphere of near joviality prevailed, while the poor deceased, laid out in splendor, slumbered nearly unnoticed amid fragrant bouquets of pale pink roses, peach and white gladiolas, and purple and yellow mums.

Many of the Czech funerals were secular affairs, not conducted in a church but in a funeral home. Not all the Czech immigrants were Catholic. The ancestors of some had joined a "reform" or "evangelical" church in the Old Country, while others, once away from their homeland, decided to free themselves from any church affiliation.

During these secular funerals, certain familiar music was expected and invariably would be heard. An organist would begin with soft melodies from the composers Smetana and Dvorak. Smetana's "Moldau" was generally favored, and then a lady, accompanied by the organist, would sing the "Going Home" theme from Dvorak's New World Symphony. Sometimes a duo or trio of Czech women would sing a Czech hymn: "*Aby Nás Pán Bůh Miloval*" ("May God Love Us"). The hymn-singing and especially the "Going Home" theme would set Mrs. Blaha off again, and her loud crying would be heard far above the muffled weeping of the mourning family. After the funeral service came the slow ride to the cemetery. Every car had its headlights on; the procession was led by a policeman on a motorcycle. The funeral cortege would be a long one, for every Czech family knew most of the other Czech families in the countryside or city, and they all wanted to be in attendance at the funeral of a deceased Czech. It was not just a wish to pay their last respects to the dead which influenced their presence. Funerals were regarded as social events on a par with weddings and family reunions, although of a more somber nature.

Rudy, Mary and Ella—late 1930's.

The old Czech Cemetery was bordered by farmland and woods where my father knew the best spots to hunt for mushrooms. As a youngster he had learned from his immigrant father where the best ones flourished, for Czechs are great mushroom-lovers and can scout them out anywhere. The area of woodland bordering the cemetery was Dad's favorite place for hunting *houby* (pronounced HOE-bee), the Czech word for mushrooms.

After clambering over an iron fence in back of the cemetery, my father, mother, and I would spend a September Sunday afternoon trudging through the colorful, rustling woods on a mushroom-hunting expedition. Dad seemed to be following no discernable path in his wanderings; as a child I was afraid he would lead us ever deeper into the woodlands and we would be lost forever. He laughed at my fears, reassuring me that he knew just where we were.

"I've been hunting mushrooms in these woods since I was a kid," he would tell me.

The mushrooms we gathered here were known by a specific name: *Václavky*, for the feast day (September 28) of Saint Václav, also known as good King Wenceslas, the patron saint of Bohemia. My dad picked those, and only those, special *houby*. Mother and I had to submit each mushroom we picked for his scrutiny. If he was unsure of one, he would look it over carefully and sniff it—if this crucial test was passed, it was added to the growing pile of brown fungi already in our basket. I never had any fears about eating the mushrooms we picked and never heard of anyone who had become ill from eating those gathered in our area.

Following a mushroom-picking afternoon, there would be no stopping off at the Blahas' Five Mile Road Tavern, for we were eager to be on our way home with our prized pickings. Our supper was a simple one. After we had prepared the mushrooms by scraping carefully with knives and cleaning gently with damp cloths, Mama would sautee them with onions in butter. We ate them with rye bread and vegetable soup or a salad, accompanied by coffee and perhaps maple nut ice cream, my favorite, for dessert. It was a satisfying meal, one that I always looked forward to every September.

After supper there would be Jack Benny to laugh at on the radio, and sometimes his nemesis, Fred Allen. Comedy programs like these helped me put aside thoughts of those terrible Monday mornings which began the five weekdays of school, five days of prison to me after the freedom of summer.

In bed Sunday night, I would live the afternoon over again in my mind. How beautiful the Cemetery Road was, I thought. It wound on and on through the gentle countryside, up and down, past fields and forests... My thoughts became a dream and in my dream I walked through a woodland of tall trees. I found a huge mushroom and ate it like a piece of maple candy. Mrs. Blaha came over to me, crying uncontrollably, and Jack Benny sat up in a tree and laughed at us.

Early Dissipation

Every year our elementary school held a "candy sale day." Mothers were asked to prepare a batch of their favorite candy to be brought to school and sold to students. Proceeds from the sale were used for special events or supplies not covered in the school's yearly budget, such as field trips, costumes for plays, extra large paper for art projects, or colored chalk to liven up our blackboards.

Mama was not much of a candy cook. Her fudge would not set properly and was either runny or grainy-textured, and her peanut brittle was too sticky. Her divinity was hardly divine—it would end up as a frosting on whatever she had on hand, whether it was cookies, left-over cake, or even kolaches.

Mama did manage to turn out a simple candy made of milk, sugar, and vanilla. When this cooked mixture hardened after being poured into a large baking pan, she cracked it into pieces, put it into a clean paper bag and told me to take it to school as her contribution. Not many of the children wanted to buy Mama's candy—only those who had to stretch their pennies as far as they could, such as Patty, for example.

Patty lived a couple of blocks down the street. One winter noon-time when some boys were chasing a few of us girls on the way home for lunch, we ran to Patty's house for refuge from their snowballs. Her mother, sitting at a table, was drinking coffee and smoking. She wore a long housecoat, her hair wasn't combed, and she looked sleepy, as if she had just gotten out of bed.

This was a new experience for me. I thought all mothers were up and dressed early in the morning. A mother who was still wearing her housecoat at noon! When I told Mama about it, she laughed and said, "There are all kinds of mothers in this world. Some get up early and make their family's breakfast, and some don't like to. But don't make quick judgment. Maybe Patty's mother wasn't feeling well so she got up late."

Some of the girls in my class were quick to make judgments about Patty, however, whispering very bad words which I never heard at home, although I knew they meant something pretty awful.

Patty, who looked a lot like Shirley Temple, blond curls, dimples, and all, was intrigued by two subjects—what boys looked like in the altogether and how babies came to be. Her conversations were mainly limited to these matters and she never missed an opportunity to volunteer her knowledge about them. Actually she had things a bit confused most of the time and technically impossible, so any information that I received from her had to be later discarded as fantasy.

Mama never talked much to me about the "facts of life." Conversations dealing with the subject seemed to embarrass her, and no doubt she sincerely believed that the less said about it the better. But Patty was always around, eager to impart some misinformation. She was the only girl I knew who associated with Jane. I once heard Audrey's mother warning Audrey about Jane: "If I catch you going near that girl's house I'll tan your bottom so bad you won't be able to sit down for a week, and I mean it!"

Neighborhood talk had it that Jane's mother was a "bad" woman and that Jane was following in her footsteps. Jane was two years older than the other children in our class and in fourth grade looked like she could already pass for sixteen. She was sleepy-eyed, bored in school, and never knew the answers when called on by a teacher. She dropped out of fifth grade, and we didn't know what had happened to her, although Patty started a rumor that Jane had "done bad things" and was going to have a baby. But we tended to discount Patty's gossip because she had a reputation for getting the facts wrong, especially facts about reproduction.

Nevertheless we were able to deduce that something unusual was amiss with Jane, because when Miss Bryan was asked about her, she blushed, looking embarrassed, and said she didn't know for sure. We were quickly given a test on division and multiplication.

Back in those days most housewives, Mama included, were alert to what was occurring in their neighborhoods. If something unusual was happening, if a household appeared out of the ordinary, if children seemed neglected, a lively back-fence conversation would take place between ladies who considered themselves to be normal, mainstream, and upholders of "the right way to do things." Talking about the situation seemed to be as far as it went; no one wanted to interfere in another family's affairs, even when such drastic measures would have been justified.

My mother didn't like to engage in gossip; she would often tell me, "Don't say anything about somebody if you can't say something nice." When the woman next door, notorious for her gossipy ways, told Mama that one of our recently-widowed neighbors was "keeping a concubine," Mama could barely keep a straight face.

"She is reading *Good Earth* and gets China mixed up into our neighborhood," Mama told me later. The supposed "concubine," a fat, kindly woman who came to help raise the deceased woman's two small daughters, was a godsend to the bereaved husband and became an excellent surrogate mother to the girls. When this housekeeper eventually married the widower, our next-door neighbor was heard to remark: "Well, at least he's made an honest woman of her!"

Certainly some of my schoolmates lived deprived, unhappy lives; cruelty, abuse, and drunkenness were no doubt commonplace in these homes. But the rules were "mind your own business" and "don't mess in other people's lives."

We never learned what had happened to Jane; and Patty, our link to the seamy side, moved away to another part of town after sixth grade. I saw her several years later, window-shopping downtown. She still looked a lot like Shirley Temple, but now she was taller, fatter, and quite pregnant. She was walking along with a pleased smile on her face. I really felt glad for her, because it was apparent that she had finally got all the facts, and I supposed that was why she looked so happy.

Even before Patty came on the scene there were other persons who were willing to give out some information and reveal something provocative and interesting. In the early grades "Small Paul" Paulson was one of these precocious individuals. He was persistent and determined, but much to his disappointment no one took him seriously. A rat-faced little boy who never looked quite clean, he sometimes smelled as though he had needed a bath for some weeks. This may have been true, because his mother must have had a hard time keeping him and his twelve siblings in a condition always fit to be seen and smelled. He was another of the few children who would buy Mama's candy, probably because the teachers always priced it so low.

Small Paul's favorite trick would be to jump out of the bushes in front of a girl, or even a group of girls—he wasn't finicky—take a bold stance, and say: "I'll show you mine if you'll show me yours!"

We would react by yelling, "Yech! You get away, smelly Paully," or "I'm telling Teacher!" or some such thing, and then we'd run away, squealing and pretending we were gagging. Nobody was silly enough, or curious enough, to take little Paully up on his dare, but he kept trying. Later, in fourth grade, one of the girls said that Patty had found his offer tempting enough to succumb to his inducement, but we never knew for certain. Considering Patty's interests at the time, it may well have been true.

What we did find out for sure was that Small Paul had been sent to the Principal's office one day and stayed there a long time, squirming in a chair, while he was given a chastising lecture about his reprehensible behavior. It seems that Miss Mallow, a tiny woman who came twice a week to instruct us in Art Appreciation, had been mistaken by Small Paul, hidden in the bushes, for one of his intended victims. He pounced out as usual and yelled his habitual challenge before realizing his error.

The diminutive Miss Mallow, shocked to her delicate bones, red-faced, but showing true valor, swatted him with her umbrella and chased him a good distance down the block. She was later able to identify him, no doubt aided by his odor, and our Principal took charge of it from there. I believe Small Paul ceased his ambushes from that time on.

Billy Altenbergen was another boy who would stoop to buy Mama's candy. He liked to follow the girls around and make them mad, although his teasing took a different form than that of Small Paul. He was a few years older than the rest of the class; we didn't know, and he wouldn't say, whether he had been held back in the early grades or had simply started school late. He wasn't slow-witted, that was certain, for he possessed an almost adult sense of humor and a sarcastic wit which he could spew out in order to make fun of his younger classmates. For this reason he wasn't popular with anyone, boys or girls. Much to my annoyance he often chose me as the object of his attentions and waited his chances to accompany me home. He would laugh at my girl friends, ask me questions about my interests and plans for the future, and tease me about my shyness. Once he told me that his father could understand and speak a little Czech and asked me if I knew that there were some Czech words that sounded like dirty words in English. I knew this was possible, provided the Czech words were pronounced carelessly, but I pretended indifference. I simply did not want to get involved in a conversation about dirty words with Billy Altenbergen.

On Valentine's Day he would put five or six mushy cards for me in the big red and white crepe-paper-covered box that sat on the edge of Teacher's desk. He would sign them "Your True Love" or "Forever Yours" or "Always Waiting" and then just his initial "B", never his name. I wasn't flattered; I was just annoyed. Some of the girls thought he was cute, with his short curly brown hair, big brown eyes, and long brown eyelashes, but I thought he was nothing but a bother. I just wanted Billy Altenbergen to leave me alone.

By the end of fifth grade I was sick of him. That year our teacher, Miss Bryan, had arranged our seating in a haphazard way and not alphabetically as usual. It happened to be my misfortune that Billy sat behind me. He naturally took advantage of this opportunity and became a total pest. Not a day went by when he didn't find some way to tease me—either by pulling my hair, tickling my neck, jiggling his desk so that my desk would also jiggle, or making funny remarks under his breath which only I could hear.

One day Billy had been more of a pest than usual; I was out of temper and ready to get even with him, but I didn't know just what to do. Then I suddenly got an inspiration.

At that time our desktops had sunken inkwells which our teachers would periodically refill from a large container of blue-black ink. We would then carefully fill our fountain pens from these inkwells, for our teachers became very upset at spilled ink.

When Miss Bryan stepped out of the room I saw my chance. Hardly thinking about what I was doing, I tore my pink ink blotter into many tiny pieces, quickly turned around, and dropped them into Billy's inkwell. Then I turned back to my book, my heart pounding so hard I was sure the whole class was aware of it.

Miss Bryan returned to the room at that moment and told us to prepare for our next lesson, which was Penmanship. Ever since second grade we were drilled in the "Palmer Method" of hand-writing. Daily we endured practice sessions to perfect the beautiful, precise circles and loops and slanted lines which were essential in the Palmer Method. It all seemed to be aimed at making everybody's handwriting look like everybody else's, all slanting to the right at just the proper angle. It must have been torture for those whose handwriting had a natural tendency to slant backward, and I can't even imagine what it did for the left-handers.

We got out our pens and filled them. I knew that Billy was struggling with his inkwell, for he was muttering bad words for my benefit. I didn't care what happened, I told myself; all I knew was that I had caused Billy some trouble, and soon Miss Bryan would notice something.

It didn't take long.

"Billy Altenbergen! Just what are you up to?"

Miss Bryan was walking from the front of the classroom to Billy's desk. I had been keeping my eyes down, but now I had to look up and turn around to see what was happening. Miss Bryan's usually calm face had a horrified expression. "You clean up that mess right now, Billy! And I mean right now!"

Billy was digging into his inkwell with his pen, bringing up clumps of ink-soaked blotter and depositing the soggy blue-black gunk on his desk top.

"Whatever got into you, Billy, doing such a thing! Look at that mess! Why did you do that?"

My heart was thumping madly as I looked at Billy.

Billy stared straight at me with those big, brown, long-lashed eyes, and then he looked up at Miss Bryan and said, "I don't know. I just don't know."

"You don't know! Well, Billy, you're going to stay after school and give that inkwell and your desktop a good cleaning. And while the rest of the class is doing their penmanship lesson, you go up to the board and write 'I will not drop paper into my inkwell' twenty times. And you'll do that twenty times after school too! In ink and in your best penmanship!"

Billy did as he was told while the rest of us practiced our Palmer loops and circles and slanting lines. My hand was shaking so much that I couldn't do the loops properly, and I was glad Miss Bryan didn't ask us to hand in our papers that day.

I knew I should have been grateful to Billy for taking the blame for something that I had done, but his past teasing, his sarcasm and annoying jokes had turned me against him. I felt no sympathy for him as he laboriously wrote his words of punishment over and over on the blackboard. If Miss Bryan had at that moment asked me if I was responsible for stuffing his inkwell, in my heartless frame of mind I would have lied gloriously and loudly proclaimed my innocence.

Not for me the gracious and admiring devotion of Mark Twain's Becky Thatcher. We were at that time reading *Tom Sawyer* in class. A chapter in the book describes how Tom takes the blame when Becky has accidently torn a page of the teacher's prized anatomy book. Unwilling to see her punished, Tom proclaims "I done it!", receives the punishment that Becky would have been given, and has to stay after school. But if Billy expected me to act like little Becky in the story "...who would wait for him outside till his captivity was done..." and afterward tell him adoringly "...how could you have been so noble!" he was sadly mistaken.

While we were putting our books and papers away, after being dismissed from school that afternoon, all I said to him, under my breath and with a mean look, was "It serves you right!"

I hurried home and left him alone with Miss Bryan and his twenty additional sentences of punishment to be neatly transcribed in the Palmer Method.

He never tried to get even, although it was out of character for him not to. The following year he bought Mama's candy as usual, and on Valentine's Day I got funny cards from President Franklin Delano Roosevelt, George Washington, Joe Louis, Abraham Lincoln, and Laurel and Hardy, and several terribly mushy cards signed with the names of boys who would never have dreamed of sending me mushy cards. Of course I could tell by the handwriting who had sent them all.

The next year we entered Junior High School, and Billy seemed to disappear from the scene. I think he was assigned to another homeroom, and I don't remember him in any of my classes. Later he moved away. I heard nothing about him until I was in Senior High, when someone told me he had joined the Navy. He must have made a nice-looking sailor, with his brown curly hair, big brown eyes, and long eyelashes. I wish I had seen him dressed in his Navy Blues.

Uncle Wence's Strawberry Patch

In my home state of Wisconsin, by the shores of Lake Michigan, a truck farmer often has a portion of his acreage in strawberries, which grow well in that humid and temperature climate. My Uncle Wencil always made a good part of his farm's income from his strawberry patch, but when World War Two came, Uncle was in a bad situation. His two youngest sons had been drafted, while his eldest son worked twelve hours a day in a factory turning out army equipment. Most of his regular hired helpers had taken lucrative war plant jobs, and poor Uncle was left without enough helping hands to pick his berries.

"Wence, you'll just have to get busy and train some new pickers," my father told his older brother. Dad then suggested my mother and me as likely prospects, along with a few other relatives and neighbors.

So Uncle Wence set out to recruit his city relatives and their friends as substitute field hands. He craftily implied that we would be aiding the war effort by joining his army of pickers, and he assured us that we would have ample opportunities to pick berries for shortcakes and pies.

Helping the war effort and getting plenty of free berries were irresistible inducements for any true blue, red-blooded, strawberry-loving Americans. Mama and I patriotically signed up for a tour of duty in Uncle Wence's strawberry patch.

A few days later, on a sunny June morning with a gray haze low in the western sky that promised a scorcher, Uncle Wence drove up in his dusty red pickup truck.

"Good morning! Good morning! Get in! Nice day for picking!" Uncle announced.

"Are we going to ride in back of that old truck?" Mama asked, incredulous.

"Sure! Don't have a bus!" Uncle laughed.

So that swaying old red pickup became our transport to and from the farm. During that first five-mile ride, all rattles, bumps, and shudders, I felt exhilarated by the speed, the fresh clean smell of country air, and the promise of a new adventure. It would be a wonderful vacation job.

We were a motley bunch of recruits. In addition to my mother and me there were my Aunt Clara and her five-year-old son Dave, our Czech neighbor Mrs. Teply and her day-dreaming son Willie, as well as several assorted teen-age neighbor boys who viewed it all as a lark.

Uncle eyed the boys with suspicion. "You kids better pick the way I tell you to pick or you can walk home," he threatened, and he meant it. He was a tough top sergeant, and the boys realized they better behave.

That first morning Uncle Wence explained the proper way to pick strawberries. Only firm, ripe red berries were acceptable—no white, underripe ones; no purple, mushy ones; no leaves, no long stems, no dirt. We were each given a large low-sided square box with four short legs and a handle. Into this box went four quart-size strawberry boxes. For every four well-topped quarts we were given a ticket. Then at the end of each day our tickets would be counted and entered into Uncle Wence's ledger. We would receive our pay when the strawberry season was over. I considered myself lucky if I could earn a dollar for each day of picking, but at that time, to someone not yet in high school, it seemed a small fortune.

I found out that everyone develops his favorite style of picking. Some are kneelers; others like to squat; some bend from the waist; and some prefer to sit in the straw while propelling themselves along on their haunches. I found a combination of positions worked best for me, because, if one set of muscles fatigued, I would just switch to another position until those got tired. And how those muscles ached that first day!

As the sun rose higher, I was glad to be wearing a cotton blouse with sleeves that could be rolled down for protection against the hot sun. Mama had also insisted I take along a sunhat.

The monotony of the work made dreamy twelve-year-old Willie feel even dreamier, and his mother's voice could be heard urging him on: "Veelie, peek! Peek, Veelie, hoory up! Veelie, be queek! Peek, peek!" But poor Willie, poetry in his soul, preferred to sit and gaze at the distant cool green woods, shimmering in the sunshine. He did not like to pick, and nothing in the world would make him hurry up and be quick.

Little Dave started to cry and was sent to sit under a tree at the edge of the berry patch. Because he was too young to pick berries properly, he was given an empty box and told he would get a penny for filling it with anything he wanted, except berries, of course. Dave happily picked white clover, red clover, dandelions, worms, a dead bumblebee, a small frightened toad, as well as various leaves and blades of grass. He got his penny, another empty box, and set out to earn some more. It was a good way to keep him occupied and out of our way.

Promptly at noon Uncle Wence blew a whistle and we all trudged down a rutted dirt road to his house, where Aunt Angeline had spread a white tablecloth over the dining room table. We were invited to wash up and then sit around to eat the lunches we had brought in paper bags. As a treat on our first day of picking, Auntie served us good fresh farm milk and wedges of her famous baked strawberry pie. For most of us, it was our first experience of hard, back-bending farm labor, and we were glad to rest our muscles and straighten our backs.

By one o'clock that afternoon we were in the berry patch again, but without the enthusiasm of the morning. It got hotter. Perspiration trickled down my neck, my sides, my back. The straw felt prickly, and no matter what position I took—crouching, bending, kneeling, or sitting—it was all uncomfortable. Insects droned. Mrs. Teply kept crooning away: "Peek, Veelie! Peek! Peek! Veelie!" The sun blazed down. Finally someone's parched voice pleaded: "Water!"

Uncle Wence came toward us with a gallon jug of water. We were grateful for the cool, refreshing, clean taste of it. I think I knew then how a tree must feel in a rainstorm, after a long drought.

By four o'clock we had covered the entire patch, and Uncle called a halt. We wearily stacked our boxes, counted our tickets, and sat under Dave's tree, fanning ourselves with our hats. Uncle marked totals in his ledger and nailed down the last of the crates.

"No picking tomorrow," were his welcome words. "We'll pick again in two or three days. Depends on how fast they ripen."

If I felt stiff and sore that evening, the next morning brought a new revelation. I could barely move out of bed. Every muscle seemed to be screaming in pain.

"Oh, my gosh, am I sore!" I complained at breakfast.

My dad, who had been born and raised on a farm, laughed. "Now you know what real farm labor is like," he said.

When I closed my eyes for a nap that afternoon, all I could see were red strawberries hiding among lush green leaves. I could even smell their sweetness. "Strawberries, strawberries," I thought wearily.

"My muscles are sore from picking strawberries, and even with my eyes closed I see nothing but strawberries. I'm sick of strawberries already."

"I can't go back to that berry patch tomorrow," I wailed. "I just can't!" Mama sympathized with me because she was stiff and sore too, but she never complained. "Think of all nice berries we can pick for pies and shortcake," she reminded me. "Don't give up ship!" Recalling Uncle's patriotic recruiting speech, she added: "Be good soldier!"

The next day Uncle Wence drove up in his truck and off we bumped back to the farm. Once down in the patch my muscles seemed to limber up. The following days brought fewer and fewer aches. June turned into July, the Fourth came and went, and still we kept picking. The weather stayed perfect for an ever-ripening supply of luscious berries. I could feel myself growing stronger and my whole body getting firmer. I got a nice tan, a bigger appetite, and I think I grew two inches that summer.

Finally at the end of the season all the pickers were allowed to pick a crate of berries for themselves. Mama baked pies and shortcakes, canned preserves and jelly, and steamed up the kitchen cooking strawberry-filled dumplings. I sat at the kitchen table for hours, picking over the berries, cutting off stems and mushy spots.

It had been hard but healthy work, and that first summer in Uncle Wence's strawberry patch left us all with a strong respect for the hard work that keeps a farm running. Strawberry picking had got into our blood. Despite the memory of our aching muscles, most of us signed up for another tour of duty the following summer, and for many summers after that.

Thank You, Miss Schneider

When I was ten years old my parents finally granted my most fervent wish—they bought me a piano. I had been begging for one ever since the age of six; now at last it stood in all its solid brown majesty under the "piano window" in our living room.

That square walnut upright was the best bargain in second-hand pianos that the want ads could produce. Sixty-four dollars, including a bench. It seemed an enormous sum to me at the time and caused my father to heave many a sad and resigned sigh. He could never understand why I wouldn't have been just as happy with a harmonica.

Now that I had the piano, the next step would be to get a teacher. The want ads again? We watched the newspaper for a few nights, but no bargain offerings in piano teachers appeared.

I questioned Carolyn, who was already "taking." She had great praise for her teacher, a Mr. Palmer Grant.

"He charges 90 cents, and you have to go to him because he won't come to your house," she said. "But my mother says he's the best. I can play 'Glow Worm' already."

Carolyn could afford the best, coming from a well-to-do family. I felt sure I would have to resign myself to second best, or maybe even third.

We borrowed the neighbors' phone directory and searched the pages for piano teachers. Mr. Palmer Grant's advertisement was the biggest of all. "Individual piano instruction in large, *moderne* downtown studio," the ad read. "Master of Music Education. Composer. Certified."

Adding bus fare to go downtown and back would bring the price of each lesson to a dollar, so Mr. Palmer Grant in his large, *moderne* studio was out of the picture. "A dollar a week!" my father groaned. "For crying out loud! You think I'm made of money?"

And then, as can be expected in life, the unexpected happened. My piano teacher came looking for me—right into the schoolyard at recess time. A strange-looking, big woman in a long brown coat, her gray hair worn short under a funny, brown Robin Hood hat with a red feather. Surrounded by children, she was handing out cards from a bulky briefcase. As she came nearer, I saw there was something odd about her eyes. One eye bulged out and seemed to be gazing off to the side. She walked stoop-shouldered among us, giving out her cards. I held out my hand for one and her good eye looked directly at me.

"I'm a piano teacher," she said. Her voice was surprisingly soft, almost a whisper. "Do you have a piano?" I nodded. "Do you take lessons?" I shook my head. "Then give this to your mother." She handed me the card and moved on, giving out more cards and asking smirking, embarrassed, or laughing children if they wanted to take piano lessons.

I looked at the card in my hand. It was neatly typewritten: "Alma Schneider. Piano Lessons. Your home or mine. 50¢ a half-hour. Experienced. 1819 Cramer Street. Call Jackson 8-4062."

The next day my mother phoned Jackson 8-4062 and my piano lessons began.

For the next five years, summer heat or winter snow, sunshine or thunderstorm, Miss Alma Schneider appeared at our front door at 4 p.m. every Tuesday. She would be wearing her long brown coat (except for the hottest summer days, when she left off her coat and appeared in a long brown dress) and her funny hat (which she covered with a shawl in winter). Striding heavily across our living room, ducking her head to avoid bumping our chandelier with her Robin Hood hat, she would gratefully accept the chair my mother offered her, fix me with her good eye, and the lesson would begin.

The simple pieces at first, with much patience on her part and much determination on mine. "The Waltz of the Teddy Bears." "The Dance of the Buttercups." Easy exercises to make the fingers nimble. Gradually the harder exercises. A Beethoven march. A theme from Chopin.

She was strict. "No! Over again! Once more!" She wouldn't let any errors pass by. If I had to play a phrase ten times before it came right, then she waited while I played it ten times. It had to be played correctly before she would let me continue.

Always expecting a little more than what I thought I could achieve, she gave me confidence by her own confidence in me. She praised me when I did well and pasted gold stars on pieces mastered to her satisfaction. I loved those gold stars and worked hard for them.

An exceptionally well-performed lesson would bring a special reward of a few big peppermints wrapped in blue cellophane.

When it came time to learn a new piece or begin a new exercise, she would play it for me first, “so you’ll know how it should sound.” She played well. Her large strong hands moved confidently over the keys. Even with my inexperience I realized that although she was not a great artist, she was certainly an able musician.

It had taken Mama and me several weeks before we were certain that she was almost completely deaf. She knew how to dominate the brief polite conversations before and after a lesson, speaking in her usual soft, almost whispered monotone, praising my progress, admiring with her good eye the pretty crocheted doilies and embroidered tablecloths my mother was so fond of stitching. Always moving on to new topics, she wouldn’t give us much chance to comment or ask questions.

But even though her ears rejected human voices, they accepted the tones of a piano with acuity. She could hear every note; and when our piano needed tuning, she would softly advise my mother to have it done.

My mother felt sorry for her and served her iced lemonades and cottage cheese kolaches in summer and hot tea and poppyseed kolaches in winter. “That poor woman,” Mama would sigh, after a lesson, “with that crooked eye, and being deaf besides. What does she have in life? Nothing but teaching piano. Just be sure to say ‘thank you’ to her when she leaves.”

And so at the door after she had received her half-dollar—“Thank you, Miss Schneider,” from me, and “Thank you, Miss Schneider,” from my mother. We were never sure if she heard.

When I started junior high school I began to have opportunities to compare my piano playing ability with that of my classmates. We had music class twice a week, and anyone who played the piano was encouraged to perform. I realized with a shock that I was a good pianist, better than most students in my class.

Somehow I had long ago surpassed Carolyn, who still “took” from Mr. Palmer Grant. He had a large, fashionable clientele and often gave recitals. Carolyn had already played in several. She invited me to attend one where I had my first privileged look at the elegant Mr. Palmer Grant, who sported a pencil-line mustache and actually wore a cape. Unfortunately, the performances of his pupils did little to justify all this elegance.

I wondered why Miss Schneider never gave recitals. “It costs too much money to rent hall for evening," Mama said. "Poor Miss Schneider, I don't think she have many pupils, if she is going around to schoolyards to hunt for them."

Once Miss Schneider gave a party for her students, and about fifteen of us showed up. I had no way of knowing how many more pupils she had, if any. She lived in an old, two-story Victorian-type house in a formerly genteel, now rundown section of our north side, not far from my home. Her younger sister, a pleasant-faced woman in her forties who worked as a secretary, lived with her. They rented out the upstairs flat to a family whose daughter was one of Miss Schneider's pupils.

The party was a short one; we played games and won cheap little prizes and then were served ice cream and cake on faded china plates. Now I could understand why this was not a teacher who would give recitals in a big rented hall and bow to the applause of pleased parents. This was a teacher who taught only those who could not afford to pay more than the little she asked.

One day my music instructor in junior high school called me aside after class and asked me how long I had been taking piano lessons and who was my teacher. He looked blank when I said, "Miss Alma Schneider."

"I don't think I know her...but you seem to have some talent, and you might consider advanced study with Palmer Grant some day soon. He's the best in town, you know, for piano."

I could picture Mr. Palmer Grant with his silly little mustache and that affected cape. I knew I could never sit through one of his lessons without breaking up and laughing, no matter how good his reputation.

Carolyn had her own opinions about Miss Schneider: "But how can you stand to look at her? That awful eye! She's so funny-looking!"

"No funnier than your fancy Mr. Pomegranate!"

The truth was that I had long ago accepted the swollen, sideward-turned eye as simply a part of Miss Schneider. I took it for granted like her long brown coat, Robin Hood hat, and her bulky briefcase stuffed with sheet music, exercise books, peppermints, and boxes of gold stars.

Twice a year our school held "musical assemblies," featuring performances by students who played any sort of musical instrument. We heard solos of clarinet, violin, piano, drum—and even those who took "tap" were asked to liven up the proceedings with some snappy tap dancing routines.

One of these assemblies stands out vividly in my memory. It was an unusual event—an assembly devoted entirely to the piano. Some music professors from a college upstate were going to act as judges, grading the performers and giving out prizes.

Carolyn confided to me that Mr. Palmer Grant had been the guiding hand behind the planning for this assembly. "He knows the judges and he knows the music superintendent. I'm glad I'm taking from him," she said. Carolyn had never progressed much beyond "Glow Worm," but she still lived in enchanted awe of Mr. Palmer Grant.

Our homeroom teacher told us on the morning of the assembly that several piano teachers had been invited to attend, allowing them a chance to hear the performances of their own and other teachers' pupils.

"Is your teacher coming?" Carolyn asked me as we took our places in the front row of the school auditorium.

"I don't know. I suppose so." I looked around at the seating area reserved for the judges and piano teachers, but I couldn't spot any funny brown Robin Hood hat.

Carolyn performed right ahead of me. She had chosen Leybach's "Fifth Nocturne" and broke down in the middle of it. Returning to her seat after having bowed to faint, polite applause, she whispered to me tearfully, "It's just too long—I couldn't memorize the whole thing." I wanted to whisper back to her that she should have stuck with "Glow Worm," but it was my turn next.

I nervously began a Spanish Dance by Granados, starting out too rapidly and keeping the pace too swift throughout. The audience, however, seemed pleased, and there was enough applause for the assembly chairman to signal for an encore. I wasn't prepared for one and frantically searched my mind for something to play. Then, desperate, hardly realizing what I was doing, I began the Leybach nocturne which had been Carolyn's downfall.

Miss Schneider had given me the nocturne to learn some months ago. A showy piece, easy to dramatize, sounding far more difficult than it was, with a lot of crescendos and runs up and down the keyboard. I finished it to a satisfying thunder of applause, and returned to my seat red-faced and happy.

Carolyn was not pleased. "That was *my* piece!" she shot at me in a loud whisper.

"I couldn't think of anything else to play and they wanted an encore!" I shot back at her.

I won a prize of some sort that day, either a book about opera or an album of Chopin etudes—I forget what it was. But my happiness was incomplete because Miss Schneider had not been there. I never even knew if she had been invited. I tried to tell her about the assembly and the prize during my next lesson with her, but as usual, it was hard to determine if she heard anything of what I was saying.

"Maybe you should write her letter," Mama told me after the lesson. "Tell her how you won prize, and how much you appreciate all she taught you."

I put off writing for some reason, and as it turned out, the letter was never written. The following week Miss Schneider did not appear for the lesson. Mama thought she might be ill, because it had been a chilly and stormy spring, and colds and flu were making the rounds. The next day Mama called Miss Schneider's number and her sister answered, saying that Miss Schneider was in the hospital with some kind of complications from pneumonia.

A few days later we read in the newspaper that my piano teacher had died after a brief illness. Sadly, Mama and I went to the visitation at the funeral home. We spoke briefly with the bereaved sister, who said that Miss Schneider had caught a bad chill in a snowstorm while waiting for a bus after a piano lesson. She had insisted on going to the lesson, even though the weather was bad and the new pupil lived way across town. She had become ill upon arriving home.

I never resumed piano lessons after that. High school brought new interests, friends, and responsibilities; somehow there didn't seem to be enough time after school for piano lessons. I would have found another teacher if I had been intent on a career in music, but that had never been my goal. I only wanted to learn how to play the piano, and Miss Schneider taught me well.

Thank you, Miss Schneider. You were the best.

Irish Eyes

In junior high school my best friend Gemmy developed an obsession with all things Irish. She took to singing Irish songs, talking in an Irish brogue, and showing me pictures of haunted Irish castles in her dad's *National Geographic.* She even discovered a long-gone Irish ancestor, many times removed; this seemed to convince her that her destiny was somehow linked to Ireland. She began insisting that everyone call her Gemmy, a nickname, instead of her real name, Imogene, which she had never liked. She felt that Gemmy suited her and somehow sounded a bit more Irish.

"Ach, sure now, 'n don't you think that me face, me poor homely face, is an Oirish face, now, begorrah?" she would ask in the broadest of brogues, her gray eyes pleading for affirmation.

Coming from a Czech background, I had little first-hand experience of the Irish people and wasn't sure just how an Irish face should look. But I was Gemmy's friend and wanted her to be happy, so I said, "You bet you look Irish. You look real Irish. Like a colleen."

Actually I wasn't exactly certain just what a colleen was, although I had often heard Gemmy singing about colleens in her Irish songs.

I had said the right thing, for Gemmy smiled with delight.

"Sure 'n 'tis happy you're makin' me now," she said.

We were sitting in my living room, pretending we were having an English high tea, with my mother's Bohemian poppyseed cake as the main attraction. Mother baked this cake for various occasions—birthday parties, family get-togethers, or just to have something special to serve when I was entertaining friends. The cake was topped with her creamy raspberry frosting, which blended well with the flavor of poppyseed. While we stuffed ourselves with cake and tea, we talked about our teachers, about boys, about movie stars, and about Gemmy's collection of bone china cups and saucers, which she said came from Ireland.

"Sure, now, 'n next time you can come to my house, 'n we'll be havin' Oirish tea," she told me.

The reason for Gemmy's burgeoning love for all things Irish was her infatuation with a lad named Jack Flanigan. Handsome, blue-eyed Jack, with his gift of blarney and his leprechaun grin, had stolen her heart, and it was all she could do to keep from staring with moon-struck eyes at him all during English, American History, and World Geography classes.

But Jack did nothing to reciprocate Gemmy's adoration. In fact, he rarely even noticed her, for Jack's true loves were basketball, football, and baseball. Eventually, in an attempt to get her mind off him, Gemmy decided to turn her attention to a more rewarding and enjoyable pursuit: designing clothes for paper dolls.

Although an Irish boy named Jack Flanigan seldom looked at Gemmy, it happened that an Irish teacher named Miss O'Meara had been watching her attentively. Ancient (or so she appeared to us) Miss O'Meara, who was our Algebra One teacher, also presided over 1 p.m. study hall. She would sit up in front of the class during study period, observing us with her sharp dark eyes; often she would march up and down the aisles, looking at the schoolwork on our desks.

During our junior high school years, before we developed compassion for them as fellow human beings, we tended to judge our teachers most severely, making fun of their looks and foibles. Their personalities strongly influenced our feelings about school in general and the subjects they taught in particular. Miss O'Meara was a special puzzle to Gemmy. How could someone with a name right out of the Emerald Isle be such an impossible person?

We referred to her as "that old mummy." She was tall, thin, dark-haired, and had a quavering voice that sounded spooky and creaky, a voice that matched her wrinkly skin. That scary voice of hers could make the toughest bully in the class sit to attention and try to make sense out of "x + 6 = 20 and therefore what is the value of x."

Gemmy and I tended to be creative types, enjoying art and literature. We made up plays and acted in them. We wrote parodies of movies and best-sellers. We saw the film *Gone With the Wind* and wrote our own version of the book, calling it *Blown By the Breeze* and filling it with bizarre characters just barely resembling those in the Margaret Mitchell epic. We were certain our book was better. And we became seriously involved with the business of clothes-designing for paper dolls.

One afternoon Miss O'Meara was sitting up front in study hall, apparently absorbed in a book. Gemmy, having finished her assignment for the day, put aside her American History textbook. As she told me later, she was in no mood to begin embroidering a map of South America. (Our World Geography teacher happened to be a kind woman of vast sympathy for youthful creative urges.) Because Miss O'Meara seemed fully occupied with her book, Gemmy sneaked her swim-suited paper dolls out of her folder and began to sketch out the outline of an evening gown.

Sitting just one seat behind her in the next row across the aisle, I caught my breath at Gemmy's boldness. I looked down at the Rafael Sabatini adventure novel which was my choice for extra credit English reading, but I was too tense to read. Instead I concentrated on the narrow groove for holding pencils at the top edge of my desk. "Gemmy," I attempted to communicate with her mentally, "put the dolls away. She'll catch you at it. Gemmy, please put the dolls away. Gemmy…"

"IMOGENE!" Miss O'Meara had materialized in the aisle next to Gemmy's desk. With a grand swoop of her skinny arm, she snatched up the dolls and dress sketches and marched stiffly up the aisle. She threw all of Gemmy's creations into the wastebasket and turned to the class, a triumphant look on her weathered face. "A study period is for schoolwork and not for paper dolls!" her creaky voice announced to all.

I knew Gemmy was fighting back tears; she loved those paper dolls and was proud of her dress sketches. I returned to Sabatini, wishing with all my heart that I could be Captain Blood holding a sword to Miss O'Meara's wrinkled neck.

After dismissal from the final class that afternoon, Gemmy pulled at my sleeve and whispered dramatically, "Follow me!" She led the way down the corridor to the room where Miss O'Meara had presided over study hall. We approached the open door cautiously and Gemmy took a stealthy look inside. The room was empty. In dashed Gemmy, grabbed her paper dolls and dress sketches out of the wastebasket, and off we ran, shaky but triumphant, past the approaching janitor and out the door to freedom.

On the way home we made a vow of vengeance on Miss O'Meara—vengeance that would be executed in case we failed Algebra One, where we both stood on very unsteady ground. When we finally decided what form our vengeance would take, we couldn't look at Miss O'Meara without silently bubbling up with laughter. We constructed a large sign which, if we failed Algebra One, we planned to attach to Miss O'Meara's classroom door: "THIS IS THE HOME OF MISS O'MEARA. EVERY YEAR SHE GETS QUEERA AND QUEERA."

Fortunately for all, we passed Algebra One and were promoted to Algebra Two. Somehow we felt vindicated, for Miss O'Meara never taught Algebra Two. We assured each other that it was simply because she was not smart enough.

"Sure'n we're finished with her now, begorrah!" said Gemmy, as we sipped honey-flavored tea from her Irish teacups.

DISH NITE AT THE GRANADA

The dastardly sergeant of the Legionnaires sneers at the young man standing before him.

"Do you and your brother want to live?" he asks. "Answer me, you dog!"

The slender young recruit regards him with cool eyes, eager to give an impudent retort, a swift, cutting reply worthy of his brother Beau.

But before John Geste, played by Ray Milland, can open his mouth, a plate crashes to the cement floor. The audience explodes with merry, yet slightly guilty, laughter. Milland's reply to the sergeant, portrayed by Brian Donleavy, is lost, but no one really cares. Except for the unhappy person whose plate is broken, everyone is having a wonderful time, for we are watching *Beau Geste*, starring Gary Cooper, and this is Dish Nite sometime in the 1950's.

Back in the 40's and 50's, they gave away dishes at our neighborhood movie theater called the Granada. For the purchase of an adult ticket, which cost twenty-five cents, you would receive a dinner plate, or a cup and saucer, or a cereal dish, or a soup bowl, or a creamer, or a sugar bowl—and you would see a couple of great old black-and-white films.

No one enjoyed Dish Nite more than my mother. She was a devoted fan of the movies and credited them with helping her to learn English. When nineteen-year-old Mama came alone to the United States from Czechoslovakia, shortly after the First World War, she knew only four words in English: *yes*, *no*, and *thank you*. Small, round-faced, with an engagingly innocent smile and one thick gold-brown braid hanging down to her waist, she barely looked her age. A large basket of woven straw held her precious possessions: a few changes of homemade clothes, crocheted shawls, an extra pair of high-buttoned shoes, an embroidered tablecloth edged with tatted ecru lace, several slim volumes of Czech poetry, two tiny prayerbooks, and her grandmother's rosary of wooden beads.

After living with her Wisconsin relatives for a few months, Mama began her working life as a live-in maid. On her days off she would take the streetcar downtown to the Orpheum and watch Valentino, eyes smoldering, lacquered hair glistening, seize a terrified Vilma Banky in his fierce embrace.

"I LOVE YOU!" the caption declared.

"PLEASE LET ME GO!" the caption pleaded, as Vilma struggled to release herself from the passionate desert chieftain.

Mama, whose tastes did not run to hot-eyed Sheiks with slicked-down hair, sympathized with Vilma and added a word here and there to her understanding of English.

Movies may have been silent in those days, but the captions, brief though they were, translated the eye-rolling, overdone emoting into the words that were Mama's introduction to English literature. As the years passed she watched Charlie Chaplin take his tumbles; Theda Bara, playing the ultimate vamp, lure her captive lovers to their destruction; and Ramon Novarro, as an early Ben Hur, emerge weary, battleworn, but victorious from the famous chariot race.

By the time Dish Nites came along the movies had been talking for some time and were a bit more sophisticated. But for those middle-of-the-week showings the theater managers always offered old films, no doubt cheaply obtained. They knew the chinaware would draw the crowds. The Granada was filled on Tuesday and Wednesday evenings with patrons who sat clutching their dishes on their laps. Experienced Dish Nite goers brought shopping bags and newspapers with them, to wrap around and protect their gifts.

Double features were always shown in those days. Certain classic films, such as the 1930's *King Kong* and *Gunga Din*, came around every few years and would routinely appear together on Dish Nite. Usually the main feature would be accompanied by a "B" movie, quickly made on a low budget. This could be a Laurel and Hardy comedy, a Gene Autry western, or one of the relentlessly grim "prison pictures" from Warner Bros., redeemed by such stars as George Raft or James Cagney. And there might even be a cartoon and a newsreel.

Mama, by this time a settled matron, always looked forward eagerly to Ronald Coleman and Gary Cooper films. Ronald, whom she regarded as the ultimate in gentlemanly suaveness, made an unforgettable appearance as Sydney Carton in *A Tale of Two Cities*, where he suffered with fine English reserve and died gloriously, keeping a stiff upper lip during all the proceedings. The following week he might return as the dashing trenchcoated adventurer Conway in *Lost Horizon*, which filled the screen of the Granada's dim, Moorish-palace interior with haunting views of the distant and unreachable Shangri-La.

Gary was Mama's ideal hero—tall, handsome, softspoken, and sparing of words. A perfect man of the West, of the Foreign Legion, or even the Bengal Lancers.

Mama also enjoyed all the early Bette Davis movies, which would show up regularly on Dish Nites. Her favorite scene in *Dark Victory* was the one where big-eyed Bette, suddenly realizing she was doomed, stared hatefully at George Brent and spat out the words "Prognosis negative!" while the audience gasped, spellbound. Mama liked to imitate Bette, much to my delight. Speaking with a rich blend of rolling *r*'s and gentle *ah*'s, she always stressed the first syllable and rarely used *a*'s, *an*'s, or *the*'s, which she considered unnecessary and a little puzzling, since they have no equivalents in Czech. When Mama, attempting a Georgia drawl, acted out the Southern belle that Bette portrayed in *Jezebel*, her definite no-nonsense *r*'s got in the way, and she ended up sounding more like a belle from the south of Prague.

"My favorite in silent movies," Mama would confide in me, as we walked down the elm-lined blocks toward the Granada on a summer Dish Nite evening, "was Conway Tearle. He was so good-looking. Only actor who comes close to him today is Gary Cooper. He was wonderful in *Plainsman*!"

Mama also liked to reminisce about her life as a housemaid. "When I worked for other people I washed thousands of dishes and I have none of my own," she would say wistfully. Then she would chuckle, "Now I got plenty dishes and every week I get more at movies!"

Whenever we were about to see a movie featuring animals, such as a Johnny Weissmuller jungle epic, a horse-racing thriller, or a tearjerker about a faithful dog, Mama would be sure to retell her own special animal adventure—the tale of the Callendar's Mickey.

Mrs. Callendar had been Mama's favorite employer. She stayed four years at the Callendar home and became a valued member of their household. When my Dad came courting steadily in a big slate blue 1926 Cleveland sedan, the Callendars realized they would soon be losing their beloved maid, for in those days, when a girl got married, she would simply quit her job and become a housewife.

"But Mickey will miss you too much!" Mrs. Callendar told Mama when she announced her forthcoming marriage. Mickey, the Callendars' dog, was a terrifying mixture of German shepherd, collie, St. Bernard, and, if Mama were to be believed, the Hound of the Baskervilles. He looked and sounded as ferocious as one of Tarzan's larger beasts of the wild. When applying for her job at the Callendar home, Mama had almost fainted when the monstrous dog came rushing into the living room.

"But he won't hurt you—he can't!" Mrs. Callendar protested, as little Mama, pale and shaking, ran for the front door.

"I am afraid of dogs—I don't want work where there is dog!" Mama, desperate, struggled with the doorknob.

Mrs. Callendar caught the dog by his collar, took hold of his jaws and forced them open. "Look! He doesn't have any teeth! Mickey could never hurt anybody! He just loves people!"

Indeed, poor old Mickey was toothless and a lover of humans. Mama was soothed, took the job, and soon was pulling huge Mickey around, shaking him and calling him a "Bad dog!"—her courage a marvel to unknowing postmen, delivery boys, and ladies selling perfumed soaps at the back door.

"Mickey was no Rin-Tin-Tin!" said Mama, recalling another long ago movie hero.

Although Mama and I would arrive early at the Granada, there was always a waiting line of moviegoers ahead of us, quarters in hand, eager for the week's offering of chinaware. Standing in the lobby, we would hear the accents of many national origins—Armenian, German, Hispanic, Italian—and above all, Czech, for our northside neighborhood had been settled by many in that immigrant group. Mama liked to exchange greetings with her compatriot acquaintances and catch up on the latest news.

"Hello, Mrs. Kohoutek! Are you going to bake kolaches for next Ladies' Circle meeting?"

Mary and Ella about 1940.

"Sure, if I can find nice poppyseed. Grocery store was all out last time I look for it."

"Mrs. Polivka, how are you? Did you hear from your brother yet?"

"Only yesterday I got airmail letter. He live in Bratislava now, working in brewery."

"Vlasta! Is nice to see you again! You think movies will be good tonight?"

"No… I don't like Westerns. I only come for dishes. Soon I have whole set."

The giveaway dishes, bearing delicate floral designs, were of remarkably good quality. Mama kept several sets in her cupboard. Once a year she would take them out, wash and dry them, then put them back in neat stacks. She used them only on special occasions, such as holidays or birthday parties, always insisting that they were "too good for everyday."

Many years later, on my annual Wisconsin visit, I enjoyed taking out a favorite rose-patterned cup and saucer for morning coffee. "Mother," I would say, "I wonder what movie we saw when we got this cup…"

Mama slips on her eyeglasses, carefully picks up the cup and examines it. She smiles and winks at me. "I think, maybe," she says, her turquoise eyes shining, "Gary Cooper. In *Beau Geste*."

A Visit Behind the Iron Curtain

After my father's death in 1964, Mama remained in the family home until she reached her early eighties. When it became apparent, even to her, that she was no longer able to take care of herself or manage household duties, I persuaded Mama to move in with me and my family in Colorado. She lived with us for two years before entering a nursing home where her needs could be better met.

Mama kept crocheting until nearly the end of her life. I supplied her with balls of crochet thread, and she kept the nurses and aides at the nursing home supplied with little doilies. Her fingers remained as nimble as in her youth.

"It's all that crocheting I did when I was young," she would tell me. "My fingers always got good exercise and now they never get tired." When she lost her ability to follow directions from crochet instruction books, she made up her own designs as she went along. If the designs for her doilies were not always neat and orderly or if the finished doilies were not perfectly round but a bit lopsided, it never gave her much concern. Her crochet hook just kept dancing merrily along.

It troubled her that she was no longer able to bake her wonderful Bohemian pastries, especially kolaches. But I baked them often and enjoyed bringing them to the nursing home, where she and her friends would eat them with delight.

Many times in the past I had asked Mama if she would like to visit Czechoslovakia to see her relatives, but she always told me that she wanted to remember her homeland as it had been when she was young. She never wanted to see the changes that took place after World War II. But my desire to see the land of my ancestors became very strong, and I finally made a visit there while Mama was still in fair health, well cared for at the nursing home.

It was a most rewarding journey, in spite of the fact that at the time of my visit the country was still under Communist control. Russian soldiers were stationed here and there, "just looking," as my cousin Ota would say, when I questioned him.

Stepping out of the customs officer's cubicle at Prague's Ruzyne Airport, I was immediately surrounded by cousins, children of cousins, and friends of cousins. I recognized my relatives immediately from photos which had been sent to us over the years. The large group greeted me warmly with hugs, kisses, and a bouquet of freshly-picked flowers. My tall, gray-haired cousin Ota, son of Mama's deceased brother Ota, took charge and led the way to the parking lot. From there I was whisked across the city in his little Czech-made Skoda. Others followed in their own tiny cars.

Hungry for information about the United States, my relatives crowded into Ota's two-bedroom apartment. Many of them, I found out, listened faithfully (and furtively) to the Voice of America or BBC radiocasts.

Ota offered wine or beer. Those who had to drive declined, as the penalties in that country were very severe for anyone who drinks and drives. The Czech police could stop any car, at any time, whether in a traffic violation or not, and test the driver to see if he or she had been drinking.

A barrage of questions began. One cousin asked: "When you go from one state to another, are there frontier guards?"

They seemed surprised when I told them the only indication that you are leaving one state and entering another might be a sign with a greeting like "Welcome to Colorado!" or "Illinois, Land of Lincoln."

"And you do not need a pass to go from one state to another?" My laughing "No!" caused some unbelief and shaking of heads.

"How long did you have to work in order to afford a trip here? Of course, we know that most American wives do not work, but how long did your husband have to work to pay your way here?"

They were amazed when I informed them that a large percentage of American married women now work outside the home. They seemed to have the impression that American housewives mostly shop or play cards.

My relatives were eager to show me their country. They had carefully planned an itinerary, and I was glad to leave it in their hands.

"When you come to the United States to visit me, I'll be happy to do the same for you," I said, and they laughed—a little bitterly, of course, for we all knew that it would be very difficult for a Czech national to get permission to leave the country for a visit beyond the Eastern Bloc nations.

"Even if they let us go, do you think we could so easily afford it?" asked Ota. "Listen, I would have to work a year, even more, just to pay for my round-trip ticket." Ota was a construction laborer, but not from choice. Intelligent and well-educated, he had spoken out against the government several years before and lost a highly-placed position in one of the Ministries.

"And even then they would not let the whole family go," Ota informed me. "Somebody would have to stay behind to make sure the others would return."

My Aunt Růža, named after my grandmother, laughed. "I'm sure they would let me go and be glad of it," she said, "because then they wouldn't have to pay my pension while I was away. They'd probably be just as glad if I never came back." Then she added wistfully, "But I'm too old for such a trip."

Teta (aunt) Růža, my mother's younger sister, was nearly eighty, white-haired, her high-cheekboned Slavic face creased with wrinkles. But she was still strong, spry, and a lover of good food and good talk, both of which she served up in ample supply during my visit. As part of my itinerary, I was to visit her for a few days in her village home.

"You will like it there," she told me. "It's very quiet, we can talk a lot, and you can tell me about America."

My nine-year-old cousin Jaroušek interrupted. "Do you have Indians in the United States?" he asked. "Really? Red Indians? Do they wear feathers?"

His father, Vláďa, offered his own view of the American frontier to his son. "Do you think, you donkey, that Indians still hold up their trains? Not any more. They have all been taken to reservations and are being held prisoners there."

I realized that their image of American Indians had been formed by some old Westerns they had watched on their television. I talked with Jaroušek about Indians and could see he was disappointed that the days of the Old West are gone forever.

"Do you have unemployment in your country?" someone asked. "What percent? Here we have no unemployment. There is so much work to do, we must import workers from other countries."

"What kind of automobiles do you Americans have? How long do you have to work to afford an auto? Do most Americans live in their own homes? That is rare here, in Prague, but if you live in a small town or village, it is a different story. How much do houses cost in your country? How much did your house cost? How big is it?"

In my uncertain Czech, with the aid of a Czech-English dictionary, I tried to answer my relatives' continuing siege of questions.

We were joined by Ota's wife, Máša, sweet-faced and smiling, who had taken part of the day off from her secretarial job in honor of my arrival. She had been busy in the kitchen.

"Time for *oběd* (dinner)," she said. Czechs like to eat their main meal in the middle of the day, with a lighter meal, called *večeře*, comparable to our luncheon or light supper, served in the evening.

We sat down to a flavorful vegetable soup with mushrooms. I told them I couldn't eat much, for I had been served breakfast on the jumbo jet before landing in Frankfurt, and then another breakfast had been served on the plane which brought me into Prague.

"But that was two hours ago!" said Máša, bringing in the main course. Since it was June and strawberry season, we had strawberry dumplings topped with a grated white cheese called *tvaroh*, heavily sprinkled with sugar. Then a few tablespoons of melted butter were poured over everything. It looked, and was, delicious and exotic to the American palate, as well as very filling, loaded with calories.

"Do all Americans eat that way?" asked Ota, when he saw me holding my fork in my right hand. He was amused when I switched my fork to my left hand to cut up my food, then switched it back to my right hand. "We Czechs do it the sensible way, keeping the fork in our left hand and our knife in our right," he said. I had to admit that the European way makes more sense.

Czechs love to eat heartily. The next morning, for *snídaně* (breakfast), Máša offered a platter of sliced hard-boiled eggs; sliced red tomatoes; rolls, called *rohlíky*, which were shaped like a longer, skinnier version of our frankfurter buns; three varieties of cheese; gooseberry jam, and a dense, grey-colored, crusty rye bread. Ground-up caraway seeds, I was told, are what give the bread such a good flavor. But it was so heavy and filling that I couldn't eat more than a small slice, which Máša had liberally spread with unsalted butter. They urged me to take more eggs, cheese, tomatoes, rolls, more delicately-flavored rose-hip tea.

I asked them if they ate cereal, and they thought I was referring to oatmeal, which they call porridge. I tried to explain our packaged dry cereals to them.

"You say you eat dry wheat? I think I have heard something about this, but these things are not often found here. Dry wheat!" Ota shook his head. "You Americans hold your knives and forks strangely, and you also eat strange food!"

I was beginning to get used to my Czech relatives' forthrightness. Their conversation was not suave and nuanced. They said what they thought and asked what they wanted to know. It was a treat for them to question me, and I enjoyed answering them, adding my own questions in return.

"Why do you eat so much?" I asked them, for once as candid as they, and everyone laughed. "It is part of our national character by now," Teta explained. "Over the centuries our little country has been taken over by so many foreign powers, and there has been so much war and uncertainty and hunger. Now when we have food we want to eat all we can, for we are never sure when the days of hunger will come again."

It was all the explanation I needed. It explained a lot, maybe even

Soldiers marching toward Presidential Palace—St. Vitus Cathedral in background—Prague, 1985.

why many Czechs smoke so much and are such prodigious beer drinkers. It is a way of easing the uncertainty, the tension, of living in a country that you cannot feel is really your own.

After breakfast we set out for a tour of Prague's highlights, with Ota and Máša as guides. We went by streetcar, which they called a tramway. It is inexpensive and a good way to observe the Praguers firsthand. Upon boarding the tram, Ota explained how I must insert my ticket into a device which presses holes into the proper numbers on the ticket.

Just in case an "inspector" would come along, he said. I never saw an inspector during all the tram rides I took in Prague, but I'm sure they came around occasionally, because everyone was very careful to have a ticket or the proper pass. Senior citizens rode free, and workers needed only their identification passes.

We alighted in *Staré Město*, Old Town, and walked down what seemed to be the heart of the city, a crowded boulevard called *Václavské Náměsti*, Wenceslas Square. Modern department stores, small shops, hotels, restaurants, bookstores, banks, and travel agencies lined the wide boulevard. Most of the Czech women wore dresses in the latest styles, while the men wore business suits and carried briefcases. Tourists, sporting the usual miscellany of tourist apparel, were everywhere. We heard voices of Germany, Italy, Yugoslavia, France, England, and the United States.

This was late June, and the national gymnastic festival, the *Spartakiáda*, held every five years, would soon be attracting visitors from all over the world. My relatives and I planned to watch the spectacle on TV, rather than attend. Much more comfortable, they told me, and far less expensive.

A light, misty rain began to fall, but this did not dampen my enjoyment of the famous sights of Prague. The 15th century astronomical *orloj* (clock) of Old Town Hall, where at the striking of every hour the mechanized statues of Christ and the twelve Apostles move to survey their audience through two windows in the face of the edifice. The ancient Gothic Tyn church; the Jan Hus monument; the statue-lined 14th century bridge called *Karlův Most*, Charles Bridge, which crosses the *Vltava*, or Moldau, the river which cuts Prague in half. The imposing Presidential Palace, formerly known as Prague Castle, the dynastic seat of Czech rulers on Castle Hill. Towering St. Vitus Cathedral; tier upon tier of red-tiled roofs; and in any direction, tall spires of legendary Gothic, Baroque, or Renaissance churches.

Walking by a music conservatory, we heard snatches of song and a tinkling piano. We passed beer halls where Praguers can sit for hours over a beer or two, discussing the topics of the day. I caught glimpses of shady green courtyards of houses centuries old, where the dust of ages has darkened the facades to a dirty gray. We could smell sausages being cooked and coffee brewing somewhere.

Suddenly, behind us, we heard the rhythmic tramping of booted feet. A troop of young Czech soldiers was marching down the center of a wide street. "Recruits," said Ota. He winked and whispered to me, "Tourists will think they are Russians."

Ota asked how long our draftees must serve in the U.S. military forces and was amazed when I told him that we had no conscription of soldiers at the time. "But how do you get people into your army?" he asked, not believing when I told him about volunteers.

Young men were drafted to serve two years in the Czech armed forces, and most of them were eager to get their military training behind them before beginning a serious career. Groups of these soldiers on leave, some very young, looking homesick, strolled about the city just like tourists, sightseeing and hunting for bargains or souvenirs.

After we had been walking and gawking and snapping pictures for hours, Ota called a halt, and we entered a small restaurant. It was already past time for the large noonday meal.

"What will you have?" asked Ota, as I surveyed the menu. "I recommend some potato soup, and then *svíčková*, a beef which has first been marinated with vegetables and is served in a sour cream sauce with dumplings. You won't be disappointed."

Already familiar with the dish from earlier days, I wasn't disappointed, for it was comparable to my mother's version. I insisted on paying for the dinner. "This is my treat for you," I said, "and besides, I have to learn how to count with Czech money."

The black-suited waiter, white napkin over wrist, solemnly accepted my paper *korunas* and offered some change, which, at Ota's prompting, I waved away. Even small, modest restaurants employed male waiters; I never saw a waitress during my stay in Czechoslovakia, although women served behind counters in cafeterias.

We were careful about what we said in public. In private, my relatives joked all they wanted about the regime, the authorities, the Soviet soldiers stationed here and there. Telling jokes was a good way to relieve tension, and Czechs are masters of the art.

The next day was Sunday, a time for visiting, strolling around the city, or attending plays and concerts. Máša had obtained four tickets for an afternoon performance of a Smetana opera called "*Hubička*" (The Kiss) at the *Národní Divadlo*, the National Theatre.

Built in the 19th century, the massive, golden-roofed National Theatre is solidly impressive from the outside. Inside, historical and mythological paintings adorn the walls and ceiling of the vestibule. Busts of famous musicians and composers line the hallways and waiting rooms, the deep pile upholstery is wine red, embellishments are in gold. I felt that the elaborate decor even outshone the opera, which was a minor piece and not as well known as Smetana's famous "Bartered Bride." The music-loving audience, in their Sunday best, seemed entranced by everything, and their applause reflected genuine appreciation of the opera as well as the elegant interior of the theatre.

All during the performance of "*Hubička*" I had felt that something was lacking, something vital that belonged in the performance was absent. I couldn't quite put my finger on what it was. Then, when it was over, I realized what I had been waiting for but hadn't seen.

Where, I asked Teta Růža, back at Ota's apartment, were the national costumes—the women's colorfully embroidered blouses, the pleated and puffed sleeves? The headdresses (garlands of flowers for the unmarried girls and elaborately embroidered caps for married women), the colorful skirts over voluminous petticoats, the high red boots? Where were the men's long brown trousers, wide belts, sleeveless embroidered jackets over white shirts, the flat hats often adorned with flowers, the characteristic walking sticks?

I had seen nothing that could be remotely characterized as a Czech national costume at the *Národní Divadlo*. The clothes worn by the performers could best be described as "generic peasant"—simple, tasteful, but lacking in character or distinction.

Auntie had only an oblique answer for me. She began to talk about the last days of the Second World War. The Soviet army entered Prague as "liberators" and the American forces had been forced to remain to the west, in Plzeň, some 80 kilometers (about fifty miles) away.

"If they had come, the Americans, to Prague before the Russians, what a difference it would have made!" she said. "We heard, from people who lived near Plzeň, that the Americans shared their food with the Czechs. They gave them supplies, chocolates, canned meat...Hah! And what happened in Prague?"

Ota interrupted. "I'll tell you because I was here," he said. "As soon as the Russians came, they helped themselves to whatever they could find. If they found only bare shelves, they took the shelves! I was a boy at the time, but I saw and I heard."

"Now everything that has always been distinctive about us," Teta Růža spoke with fervor, "is being taken away little by little. Even the *Spartakiáda* is no longer what it used to be. Before the war, our gymnastic festival was called the *Slet*, and it was definitely national, a true Czech event. Now it is nothing—a hodge-podge. Only those who have never seen a real *Slet* would find this one impressive."

We talked for a long time about the events that followed the war. I could sense the longing, the feeling of loss, in their voices, particularly Teta Růža's, as they recalled the long gone days of the first Czechoslovak republic.

The following day Ota drove me to Teta's home in a small village east of Prague. In back of her crumbling old house, Auntie had a large *zahrada*, or garden, where she harvested potatoes, onions, carrots, beets, kohlrabi, cabbage, peas, beans, currants, strawberries, raspberries, and gooseberries. Most of her produce would go to nieces and nephews who did most of the garden work.

Her village consisted of one main street and one side street. There were about thirty houses, one grocery store, and a tiny post office. Most of the houses were as ancient as Teta's, with flower gardens in front and vegetable gardens in the rear. Nearly every home had window boxes displaying geraniums, petunias, or begonias. Czechs are great flower lovers, and one can see flower boxes and gardens everywhere, beautifying village cottages or Prague's apartment houses and office buildings.

After strolling about Teta's village, looking over old photo albums, and talking about family history for a few days, I was taken in Ota's Skoda to a smoky industrial town not far from the village. I would stay there with another cousin, Jana, her husband Vláďa, and their son Jaroušek, the little boy who loved Indians.

Rosy-cheeked, fat, and jolly, Jana's greatest joy in life seemed to consist in seeing that her family was well fed. She was a nurse, yet seldom mentioned her job in a nursing home. (Even now, in the newly-formed Czech Republic, most married women hold jobs out of necessity because of their husbands' low wages.) Jana's father, already deceased, was my mother's youngest brother, Zenda, the baby for whom she would go on her milk-seeking expeditions during the First World War.

With a great reputation in the family as an accomplished cook, Jana cross-examined me regarding nourishment.

"Are your markets well-stocked with oranges and bananas? Can you go there any time of day and they will have bananas? We get small oranges here, not very sweet. I don't know where they come from. Do you grow oranges in your state? How about apples? Do you have many kinds? What are your grocery stores like?"

The grocery stores I entered during my visit were small, drab places—shelves barely stocked, vegetables often wilted, and canned goods with mainly black-and-white labels reminiscent of our generic brands. In Prague there were a few open-air markets selling fresh produce from the State farms, and this always sold out quickly. In addition, a shopper had to wait in one line for fresh baked goods, another line for fruit, and yet another for vegetables. Lucky the Praguer or small-towner with a backyard garden, and I was happy for Teta Růža and my gardening cousins.

In anticipation of my coming, Jana had stocked up on large bananas and some wrinkled apples.

"Have a banana," she would say to me any time of day. "They are not always available. I saw this *fronta* yesterday, just forming, and it was my luck that they had plenty of bananas. From Cuba, I think. Eat! Eat!"

Frontas were lines which formed in front of stores whenever anything hard-to-get became available. No self-respecting Czech would ever be found outside without a *taška*, or shopping bag, just in case he or she should come upon a fronta. Scarce wrapping paper was used mainly for meat or baked goods. Anything else—apples, oranges, canned goods, bottles—was just piled into your *taška.*

The sight of so many men carrying shopping bags was unusual to me. "Men do not carry *taškas* in your country?" asked Vláďa. "But what if they are coming home from work and they see a *fronta* forming for some nice oranges? Then they will be out of luck." Vláďa, working as a laborer in a factory, seemed to consider the United States a technologically superior, but socially backward, country. "So your men do not carry *taškas*! Are they too proud?"

Jana and I discussed baked goods and the cooking of dumplings, which are quite a staple of the Czech diet. I asked her about kolaches. "Some of the older women still bake them the old-fashioned way," she said, "and some bakeries, too, but they're too much trouble and take too long for the working wife. I don't think I'd know how to make them anymore." Máša had made a similar remark back in Prague, and I felt a little depressed. This seemed like a true cultural loss. Could it be that the great Slavic art of kolach-baking would die out? I fervently hoped not. I made a mental note not to mention Jana's and Máša's words to Mama when I returned to the States. I wanted her to believe that kolaches were still baking in the ovens of all Czech housewives.

Vláďa and Jana took several days of vacation so they could accompany me on tours of museums, medieval castles and graceful Renaissance chateaus in the region of East Bohemia. After a few days I was almost overwhelmed with the beauty of those old buildings, most of which were undergoing extensive restoration by the government to return them to their former grandeur. Owned centuries ago by wealthy nobility, they were at the time of my visit referred to as "State" chateaus or castles, open to public viewing. Just to see the enormous and ornate tapestries, the exquisite porcelains, sparkling crystal chandeliers, and the graceful period furniture in these historic buildings was worth the trip to this area of the country.

The final days of my visit were spent in Prague again—meeting other relatives, gift shopping, and sightseeing. I also had to say goodbye to its famous landmarks; winding, narrow, brick-paved side streets; parks, squares, and tree-topped hills; its generous, openhearted people.

I had to cross and re-cross that marvelous old Gothic bridge, *Karlův Most*, with its procession of statues of saints and legendary heroes. I had fallen in love with it, as I had fallen in love with so much of the old part of Prague; it became to me a fairy tale city that had bound me in its spell.

My three-week visit seemed much too short. I want to return some day, I told Ota and Máša and Teta Růža at the airport. They smiled and nodded. "*Na schledanou*!" they said. "Until we meet again!"

"Tell your mother, tell my sister," said Teta finally, her eyes glistening with tears, "that I can still bake those kolaches, and if she had come here, I would have baked plenty, just to show her." She managed a smile. "But I'm certain," she added, "that your mother could bake better ones."

Mary on Charles Bridge, Prague—1985.

"Your Mother Is Not Like Other Mothers"

Now, seeing them in the perspective of time, I enjoy looking back on those tender years when Carolyn became my "best-friend" in second grade and told me something about my mother which was a revelation to me.

"Your mother is not like other mothers," Carolyn said one morning as we walked to school. "Your mother has an accent. She wasn't born here, like my mother or Audrey's mother or Janet's mother. She doesn't talk like anybody else's mother that I ever heard talk. She sounds funny."

If I had been a bolder child, I would have told little Carolyn to shut her lip. I would have told her that it was none of her business what my mother sounded like. I would have told her that I thought her mother sounded just too-too-tooty-snooty-high-falooty, and so there, too!

But I said none of those things, for I was not very bold, especially in Carolyn's presence, so I kept my mouth shut. How strange that before she revealed her valuable information to me I had never noticed Mama's accent. But afterwards I became very much aware of it. Yes, it was true. Mama did have an accent. A real, honest-to-goodness Central European accent, not as pronounced as some I had heard, but it was there. Inwardly I would shudder a little when Mama talked about *be*ginning new *sem*ester, *Thanks*giving Day, *Hall*oween party, and my *sat*isfactory *re*port card. Coming unknowingly under Carolyn's influence, I began to be embarrassed by my mother's accent. And soon, even a bit ashamed of my mother.

How nice it would be, I would say to myself, to have a mother who spoke proper English, belonged to the Women's Club, was actually a college graduate, and did interesting things like acting in children's plays on Saturday mornings at the Women's Clubhouse auditorium. How lucky Carolyn is, I would feel, to have such a mother. I became convinced that my mother never did anything important.

Maybe Mama sensed something of Carolyn's superior attitude toward me and my own confusion, because she would say to me, "You should have other girlfriends, not just Carolyn. She isn't only girl in world. Why don't you ask Janet or Owdrey to come over sometime and play?"

"Oh, Mama, please! Can't you ever pronounce anything right? It's Audrey! AUDREY! Not 'Owdrey'! Can't you ever learn?"

"All right, all right, 'Audrey' then. I can *pro*nounce it."

"Pro*nounce*!"

"All right. Pro*nounce*. Is that better?"

"Oh, Mama, you'll get it wrong again next time, I know you will!"

I went to my room, almost in tears. My mother followed me and put an arm around my shoulder. "You know, Mary, English is hard language," she said, giving me a little hug. "In Czech language, we *pro*nounce, no pro*nounce*, everything just like it is spelled. And we always know just where to put accent in word. But English—oh, that's hard language for foreigner to learn. Maybe I should go back to night school, and study some more, so I would please you, eh?"

As the years went by Carolyn and I gradually drifted out of our friendship. Her family moved to a large house in a prosperous neighborhood, and we soon saw each other only during some classes in high school. When the time came for entering the University of Wisconsin, she moved into a sorority house, while I shared quarters with two roommates in a "cooking-privilege house" off campus. We now moved in two separate worlds.

By this time I had several friends whose mothers had been born in foreign countries. There was Marie, whose German-born mother loved to treat us to cherry-and-almond stollen or crunchy streusel-topped coffee cake. Renee, from an Armenian family, had a mother who shyly refused to try to speak English in front of her daughter's college friends, in spite of Renee's urging and gentle teasing (I wondered if there had been a "Carolyn" in Renee's life too). Raquel's tiny, bright-eyed Mexican mother introduced me to tortillas and dark, delicious refried beans, all homemade. Anna's mother, when told of my Czech background, tentatively spoke a few words of Croatian to me. I answered her in Czech, and we happily discovered we could communicate in two distinct, but not dissimilar, Slavic languages.

Carolyn had been wrong, I eventually realized. My mother was not so different after all. My mother was like these mothers—women who were content to stay at home, tend the house, and keep their families happy in the best way they knew. The old-fashioned, Old Country way. Carolyn had never known women like these, with their juicy accents, their exotic cooking, and their stories of life in distant lands. She had assumed all mothers were like hers—college-educated, self-assured, at ease in American ways, coming from generations of American background. Never groping for the correct words in English, never unsure of the right pronunciation, the proper way to act…

I gradually became aware of an important similarity between myself and my friends with two cultural environments, one ethnic and one American. We all seemed to have more perspective with which to view both environments; we could be more discriminating, more able to pick the "chaff from the wheat." We could pick and choose what we wanted from both cultures, enhancing and fulfilling our lives to a greater degree than if we had only been exposed to a single heritage.

Renee summed it up one day when she said, "It must be nice to have a seventh-generation American background. Nice—but rather…limited! I wouldn't trade my little Armenian mama for all the mamas in the world!"

Ella in her twenties.

And I can say the same about my Bohemian mother. She infused my life with richness and dimension in so many ways. With reminiscences, happy and sad, of life in Bohemia. Stories about working as a bewildered maid in her new country. A never-ending supply of folk tales. The traditional, delicious Czech foods she served. The melodious folk songs that she sang so well—songs of gypsies, soldiers, farmers, village maidens in love, the gathering of crops, and promises made and never forgotten.

Mama is gone now, buried next to my father in the old Czech cemetery by the side of that country road, where cooing doves still sing their soft, liquid call. The comforting warmth of her presence will always be with me. I can chuckle when I recall her ever-ready humor and marvel at the memory of all the love shining in her blue-green eyes. I hear in my mind her sweet voice, speaking with that delightful accent, promising me that next time she will *pro*nounce, no pro*nounce*, everything right, and urging me to eat some poppyseed kolaches.

Mama taught me no favorite maxims, no wise sayings that would guide me on life's journey; she gave me only the example of a good and giving life, kindly and sweetly lived. Her happiest moments seemed to come while sharing reminiscences and serving food to her family and friends. "Eat, eat more!" she would gladly invite us all, "And while you eat, I'll tell you a story…."

Recipes

Soups

Entrees

Side Dishes

Desserts

Old-Fashioned Bohemian Soups

Milk Soup with Rice

½ cup rice
1 cup water
1 tbs. butter or margarine
2 quarts milk
Herbs (marjoram, thyme, parsley—your choice)
Salt
1 egg

In covered saucepan, cook rice with 1 cup water. When nearly all the water has evaporated, add butter or margarine, herbs and 2 quarts milk with salt to taste. Slowly bring to the boiling point. Beat one egg and add very slowly to the milk and rice mixture, beating constantly. Serves 6 to 8.

Cauliflower Soup

One head cauliflower
1 to 2 quarts water
2 or 3 beef bouillon cubes or 2 cups beef stock
2 tsp. flour
2 tbs. milk
1 tbs. butter or margarine
1 egg (if desired)
Herbs of choice

Separate one cauliflower into flowerets, wash well, and cook in 1 to 2 quarts of water to which you have added 2 or 3 beef bouillon cubes or beef stock. In another saucepan mix 2 tsp. flour with 2 tbs. milk. Gradually add some water in which cauliflower was cooked. Add 1 tbs. butter or margarine, 1 egg (can be omitted if desired), and herbs of your choice. Mix well and add to rest of cooked cauliflower and slowly bring to the boiling point. Add more milk for creamier soup, if desired.

Beer Soup

1 quart beer
1 quart water
2 tsp. sugar
1 tsp. butter or margarine
Pinch of nutmeg
2 eggs
1 cup milk
Flour if desired

Cook 1 quart beer with 1 quart water. When it begins to simmer, turn down heat, add 2 tsp. sugar, 1 tsp. butter and pinch of nutmeg. Beat two eggs with one cup of milk and add very slowly to beer mixture, stirring constantly so it will not curdle. Remove from heat before it boils. Can be thickened with flour if desired.

Lentil Soup

One ham bone with some attached meat
6 cups water
1 1/2 cups dried lentils
Dash pepper, to taste
1 large onion, chopped
1 1/2 tsp. salt, or to taste
1 tsp. brown or white sugar
3 or 4 carrots, sliced
1 bayleaf

Wash lentils in sieve and soak in cold water for about an hour. Pour off water and combine lentils with rest of ingredients in large saucepan. Heat to boiling and then simmer for about an hour or until lentils are very tender. Take out ham bone, strip off any bits of meat and leave in soup. Remove bay leaf.

If soup seems too thin, make a paste of 2 tbs. flour and a little water and add to soup. Bring to a boil, stirring carefully, until of desired thickened quality.

Some cooks prefer to soak lentils overnight instead of just one hour. I use the overnight method.

Liver Dumplings for Soup

1/2 lb. beef, pork, or lamb liver
1 small onion
3/4 tsp. salt
Dash pepper, nutmeg, and marjoram
1 beaten egg
1 tbs. melted margarine
1 cup soft bread crumbs
Meat broth

Remove any membranes from liver. Put liver and peeled onion through food chopper or use blender or food processor to chop to a fine consistency. Add seasonings, egg, margarine and crumbs, mixing well. Drop by teaspoonfuls into boiling meat broth or favorite clear soup; cover and simmer for 15 minutes. Makes about 20 dumplings. Add to any favorite soup.

Noodles for Soup

One egg
1/2 tsp. salt
About 2 cups flour

Beat egg slightly with salt. Mix in flour to make a stiff dough. Knead about 5 minutes on a slightly floured board. Roll paper-thin. Cover with a towel and let rest about 20 minutes.

Cut in 3-inch strips. Pile the strips on each other and cut in shreds or 1/4 to 1/2 inch widths.

Add noodles to favorite soup or make a clear soup using leftover beef or chicken stock. Cook in soup until noodles are soft—about 5 to 10 minutes. Soup may also be made by simply adding boiling water to beef or chicken bouillon cubes.

Entrees

Marinated Beef
(Svíčková)

3 to 5 lb. rump roast or sirloin tip roast
1 large onion, sliced
1 cup sliced celery
1 cup sliced carrots
1 cup sliced parsnips (only if desired)
1/2 tsp. pepper
1/2 tsp. thyme
1/4 tsp. dried parsley
2 bay leaves or 1/2 tsp. flaked dried bay leaf
4 cups water
1 cup vinegar
2 tsp. brown sugar
1 tbs. salt

Place vegetables, flavorings, herbs, water, vinegar, and sugar in large casserole dish. Mix well and then add meat. Cover and place in refrigerator. Refrigerate three to six days, turning once or twice a day. The longer the meat marinates, the more tender it becomes.

When ready to use, simply place casserole dish in 325° F. oven, add salt, and bake, covered, for 3 to 4 hours, adding a little water if necessary. Toward end of roasting time, add a paste of about 2 tbs. flour and a little water, to thicken. Some cooks add sour cream to meat and vegetable mixture before taking out of oven, others spoon sour cream over mixture just before eating. Still other cooks prefer not to use sour cream; instead they melt plum jelly with water in a saucepan, bringing to a boil to make a plum sauce which is then spooned over meat and vegetable mixture.

This dish is often served with dumplings, such as bread-center dumplings.

Roast Pork

4 to 5 lbs. pork loin
1 small onion
Salt & pepper to taste

Make sure pork loin is clean. Make slits in fat and stuff onion slices into slits as desired. Rub salt and pepper on roast as desired. Set oven at 350°F. and roast until meat is very tender in a deep roasting pan with cover. I keep a small amount of water in the bottom of the pan, where I have put the remainder of the onion slices. Baste occasionally with the juice which results from this water and onion mixture and the roast drippings. Roast about 3 hours or until well done. Pork roasted in this way is very moist and tender.

Czech cooks like to serve pork roast with bread-center dumplings. Sweet-sour cabbage is a good vegetable accompaniment.

Carp in Black Gravy

1 large carp (or can be any white-fleshed fish)
1/2 cup raisins
1/2 cup dried prunes with pits removed
A few crushed gingersnaps or flour to thicken
Pinch salt
1/2 cup dried apples

Place fruits in a large saucepan and add water to cover. Cook until fruits are softened, simmering for about 15 minutes. Add fish and a pinch of salt and continue to cook for about 15 minutes longer or until fish is tender. Do not overcook. Serve fish along with the fruit gravy. If a thicker sauce is desired, remove fish from saucepan and add a few crushed gingersnaps or a few teaspoons of flour slowly to the cooked fruits and cook a few minutes, stirring carefully. Pour sauce over fish.

If desired, fish may be baked or poached in oven for about 15 minutes at 375°F. and the fruit sauce cooked separately in a smaller saucepan. Pour sauce over fish.

SIDE DISHES

Bread-Center Dumplings

2 eggs
1 cup milk
2 cups flour (or more)
1 tsp. baking powder
1 tsp. salt
2 slices stale bread or toast
Melted butter or margarine

Beat eggs, add milk, and beat again. Sift flour with baking powder and salt and add to egg mixture. Stir well. If dough is too sticky, add a little more flour. Cut stale bread or toast into cubes and saute in melted butter or margarine. Stir bread cubes into dough. Bring salted water to boil in large pan, and drop dough into water by tablespoons. Cook about 10 minutes.

Plum Dumplings

4 medium potatoes, boiled and mashed until smooth
1 egg
2 cups flour (approximately)
1 tsp. baking powder
1 tsp. salt
Milk to moisten, if necessary
20 blue Italian plums
2 quarts boiling water (salted)

Add egg to boiled mashed potatoes and mix well. Gradually add 1 cup flour sifted with baking powder and salt. Add more flour gradually as needed, but not too much, as this tends to toughen the dough which should not be sticky and yet not too stiff. Add a teaspoon or so of milk if necessary to bring to desired kneading consistency. Place dough on well-floured board and knead slightly. Shape into long roll and cut off pieces large enough to form circles, which are then shaped around plums. Be sure dough is spread evenly around plum. Pinch ends together tightly.

Bring 2 quarts of slightly salted water to a rapid boil, then place about half of dumplings in water. Keep them from sticking to bottom of pan by lifting gently with a wooden spoon. Boil about 10 minutes in uncovered pan. When these are done, place rest in same water and continue as with first batch. Serve hot with brown sugar or white sugar and cinnamon.

Leftover dumplings can be refrigerated and re-heated, either in the oven in a covered baking dish or on the stove. Add a little water when re-heating.

Sweet-Sour Cabbage

1 medium head cabbage
2 tbs. sugar
2 tbs. white vinegar
Dash salt
Onion if desired

Chop cabbage coarsely after washing well. Put in large saucepan and add water to cover. Add sugar and dash salt. Add sliced onion if desired. Cover and cook over low flame about 20 minutes. Add vinegar to taste and cook a few minutes longer.

Some cooks brown the onion in a little butter and then add cabbage, water, sugar, and salt, cooking until tender and then adding vinegar.

Either green or red cabbage may be used.

Sauteed Mushrooms

1 pound fresh mushrooms
$^1/_4$ cup onion, finely chopped
$^1/_4$ cup butter or margarine

Carefully clean and slice mushrooms. Melt butter or margarine in saucepan, then add mushrooms and onion. Saute over medium heat, stirring often, for about 10-15 minutes, until onions are golden brown. Do not allow to burn. Serve with brown bread or over toast.

Mushroom Pie

Prepare mushrooms as above. After sauteing for about five minutes, add two heaping tablespoons flour, $^1/_2$ teaspoon salt, a dash of pepper and nutmeg. Slowly add $^3/_4$ cup milk and cook over low heat, stirring constantly, until thickened. Add two beaten eggs and mix all together. Pour into an 8-inch pie plate lined with plain pastry and bake at 400° F. for about 30 minutes, or until delicately browned.

DESSERTS

Mama's Old-Fashioned Kolaches

1 cup lukewarm milk
1 package active dry yeast
1/4 cup sugar
1/2 tsp. salt (increase to 3/4 tsp. if using unsalted butter or lard)
2 1/2 to 3 cups flour—more if needed
1/4 cup shortening (butter, lard or margarine; lard makes the most tender kolaches, but few of us want all the cholesterol. I use margarine.)
2 eggs

Add yeast to lukewarm milk in mixing bowl. Let stand a few minutes, then stir until dissolved. Add sugar, salt, melted shortening, and eggs to yeast mixture and mix well with egg beater or electric mixer. Gradually add flour until firm enough to knead (using large wooden spoon), adding more flour if necessary. Turn dough out on floured board and knead until elastic. Put into buttered mixing bowl to rise, and turn dough in bowl so that top of dough is buttered (I use margarine here also). Cover with a warm damp towel and let rise in a warm place (about 85°F.) until doubled in bulk (about 1 to 1 1/2 hours or more). Punch dough down firmly to remove air bubbles and then let rise again (about 1 hour). Punch down again and place dough on floured board.

Shape into cylinder as thick as your wrist. Cut pieces 1/2 inch thick off cylinder. Shape pieces into squares, handling as gently as possible. Bring opposite corners of dough together over filling and pinch all together, sealing well. Kolaches will now look like small square envelopes of dough with filling showing through near corners. Arrange kolaches about 1/2 inch apart on buttered baking dish or cookie sheet. Lightly brush tops and sides of kolaches with melted shortening (I use a combination of melted margarine and vegetable shortening) and let rise in warm place about 1/2 hour to 1 hour. Bake at 375°F. until delicately brown (15 to 20 minutes). Sift powdered sugar over kolaches and enjoy!

Some cooks complain that their modern-day electric ovens dry out the dough, and they prefer to bake in gas ovens. If you have an electric oven, you can overcome the drying-out problem by placing a small pan of boiling water in the oven during baking.

Fillings for Kolaches

Prune Filling:

Cover 1 1/2 cups dried pitted prunes with water and cook until prunes are plump and tender (about 15 to 20 minutes). Add sugar to taste. Pour off excess juice. Mash until pulpy and drain off more juice if necessary.

Apricot Filling:

Use dried apricots and follow recipe for prune filling.

Cottage Cheese Filling:

Combine 1/2 cup sugar with 1 lb. dry (not creamed) cottage cheese. Add 1 large beaten egg and dash of salt. A teaspoon of grated orange rind or 1/4 cup raisins may also be added for flavor variety. Mix well.

Poppyseed Filling:

Poppyseed must be finely ground. Use an old-fashioned coffee grinder if you have one. If not, your blender or food processor might do the job. Grind 1 cup of poppy seed. Add 1/4 cup milk and 1/2 cup sugar. Cook over very low heat for about 5 minutes, stirring constantly. Add 1/2 tsp. grated orange rind and 1/4 cup raisins, if desired. Mix well. If mixture is too thin, add a few teaspoons of finely crushed graham crackers.

Poppyseed can still be purchased in bulk in some supermarkets. Otherwise you will have to look for it in some specialty stores. Don't worry—this kind of poppyseed will not make an opium addict out of you. Czechs have been eating poppyseed kolaches for centuries without becoming addicted to the poppyseed, although one can easily become addicted to kolaches of any kind!

Nut Filling:

Beat two egg whites. Add 8 oz. finely ground walnuts and 1/4 cup sugar. Mix well. If a thicker filling is desired, add some finely crushed graham crackers.

Mama's Buchty
(Also known as Baked Fruit Dumplings or Kolach Balls)

Plum Buchty:

Use kolach recipe for dough. Let rise as in kolach recipe. Wash and dry small, ripe, Italian plums (sometimes called Italian prunes) which are found in supermarkets in September. Slit plums just enough to take out pits but do not separate halves. Put about 1/2 teaspoon of powdered sugar into center of plum (in opening where you removed the pit) and press halves of plum together. Place plum in center of round piece of dough (which you have cut off from cylinder as in kolach recipe) and work dough around plum, pressing dough together neatly and firmly to make a ball. This takes a little practice, so have patience. Arrange buchty (seam side down) on baking sheet as in kolach recipe and let rise in warm place. Bake at 375° F. until delicately brown (about 15 to 20 minutes). Sprinkle with powdered sugar. This recipe makes about 15 buchty.

Grape Buchty:

You will need a pound or two of ripe purple Concord grapes. Wash grapes and dry well. If you can remove seeds without removing too much of the pulp, do so. Otherwise you will be spitting out the seeds as you eat the grape buchty. If you are among family or close friends, this won't matter, as you will be too busy enjoying your buchty to bother about table manners. Prepare as for plum buchty—use about four or five grapes for each ball. When formed, balls will be lumpy, of course, but as they rise they will tend to smooth out. Sprinkle with powdered sugar after baking at 375°F. about 15 to 20 minutes.

Plums are a favorite fruit in Czechoslovakia and are used often in cooking and baking. In olden days many roads and private paths were lined with plum trees. It was the custom for the owners of the trees to sleep under them on the late summer nights just before they were to be harvested, because thieves or mischievous youngsters were always on the prowl to steal the ripe plums from unwatched trees.

Grape buchty are Mama's own invention, since grapes were not traditionally grown in Bohemia, where the growing season is too short. When she came to the United States, Mama discovered Concord grapes, which she often used instead of plums in her buchty.

Boži Milosti

Divine Little Doughnuts

Translated into Czech, Boži Milosti can mean God's Grace or God's Sweetness. These delightful little confections are indeed a tiny taste of heaven, but they are very rich, so don't indulge in too many!

4 egg yolks, well beaten
4 tbs. cream
2 tbs. sugar
1 stiffly beaten egg white
2 tbs. rum or whiskey
Dash salt
1 $^{3}/_{4}$ cup flour

Beat egg yolks, cream and sugar together until well blended. Fold in egg white and liquor. Add salt, 1 cup flour and mix well. Add remaining flour gradually, mixing until stiff dough is formed. Use more flour, if necessary. Roll out $^{1}/_{8}$ inch thick. Cut into strips about 4 x 1$^{1}/_{2}$ inches. Slash edges and twist slightly, or slash in center and pull one edge through center. Drop into hot deep fat at about 360° F. and fry until golden brown. Drain on paper toweling and dust with powdered sugar. Makes about 3 dozen.

Alternate recipe:

1 $^{1}/_{2}$ cups flour
1 tbs. butter
1 egg plus 2 egg yolks
3 tbs. red wine
2 tbs. cream
1 tsp. sugar
Pinch salt

Mix and knead all ingredients together until light and fluffy. Divide into four or five parts and roll each portion very thin. Cut into small oblong pieces and fry as in above recipe.

Cherry Bublanina

A Rich Dessert

$^1/_2$ lb. butter or margarine
1 $^1/_2$ cups sugar
6 eggs
2 cups cake or regular flour
2 tsp. baking powder
Dash salt
2 cups fresh cherries, or
1 can sour or sweet cherries, well drained

Cream butter or margarine and sugar, add three to six egg yolks, depending on desired richness, and beat until light and fluffy. Sift flour, baking powder, and salt. Add the dry ingredients slowly to the egg mixture. Beat the six egg whites until stiff and fold into cake batter. Pour into greased and floured 9 x 12 pan. Scatter cherries over top of dough, pressing in slightly. Sprinkle top with a few tablespoons of sugar, as desired. Bake in 350°F. oven about 30 minutes. Cool and cut into squares.

Plums, peaches, or blueberries may also be used, instead of cherries. If using canned fruit, be sure to drain well.

Poppy Seed Cake

1/4 cup poppy seeds
1 cup milk
2/3 cup butter or margarine
or other shortening
1 1/2 cups sugar
2 1/4 cups flour, sifted
2 tsp. double-acting baking powder
2 egg yolks
3 large egg whites, well beaten
1/2 tsp. salt
1/2 tsp. vanilla

Soak poppy seeds in milk overnight in refrigerator. Cream shortening with sugar until light and fluffy. Add egg yolks and mix well. Sift flour once before measuring. Sift flour, baking powder, and salt together. Add dry ingredients alternately with milk and poppy seed mixture, mixing thoroughly after each addition. Add vanilla and mix well. With rubber scraper or whisk, gently fold in stiffly beaten egg whites. Pour batter into two greased and floured 8-inch layer pans or two small loaf pans. Bake at 375°F. for about 35 minutes.

Raspberry Cream Frosting

2 cups powdered sugar
3 tbs. fresh or canned
raspberry juice
1/4 cup butter or margarine,
softened
Few drops milk

Cream powdered sugar and butter together, mixing well. Add raspberry juice and a few drops of milk. Beat until smooth.

A note about the following recipe: While strawberry pie, or any kind of pie, as a matter of fact, is not a traditional Czech dessert, Mama baked it often enough that I came to associate it with other Czech delicacies.

Due to her inclination to knead the dough, my mother's pie crusts were always tough. But the baked strawberries inside the unfortunate crusts were so good that I always looked forward to strawberry season.

Baked Strawberry Pie

Crust:

2 cups pastry flour (all-purpose flour)
1 tsp. salt and 1 tsp. sugar
2/3 cup cold shortening
1/3 cup ice water (approximate)

Mix flour with salt and sugar. Cut in shortening with a fork or pastry blender until mixture is in even pea-sized pieces. Sprinkle ice water over mixture, gradually adding by teaspoonfuls and stirring with a fork. Add just enough water so dough can be gently formed into two balls. Handle dough as little as possible and do not knead. Wrap the two balls of dough in wax paper and keep in cool place while you prepare the strawberries and sugar-flour mixture.

Filling:

About 4 cups firm, ripe strawberries, sliced in half
3/4 cup sugar (add a little more if you prefer a sweeter pie)
1/4 cup flour

Wash strawberries gently and carefully. Slice in half and set aside. Mix together flour and sugar and set aside.

Place one ball of dough on floured board or waxed paper. Roll with rolling pin with quick, light strokes. Roll out from center as evenly as possible so pastry is same thickness throughout. Roll to about 1/8 to 1/4 inch thickness.

Place pastry into 9-inch pie plate without stretching. Spoon about two tablespoons of flour and sugar mixture onto bottom of pie plate, covering evenly to sides of plate.

Place one layer of sliced strawberries into plate, and sprinkle generously with flour and sugar mixture. Repeat with another layer of strawberries and sugar and flour mixture. Brush edge of lower pastry layer with water.

Roll out second ball of dough and place over berries. Press onto moistened lower edge and crimp. Pierce top layer of pastry with fork to let steam escape. Bake at 375° F. for 45 minutes to 1 hour.

Pronunciation of Czech Words

Vowels are pronounced as follows:

Short *a* as in artist
Long *á* as in arm
Short *e* as in bet, nest
Long *é* as in there
Short *ě* as in yet
Short *i* as in it
Long *í* as in machine
Short *o* as in thought, caught
Long *ó* as in nose (seldom used)
Short *u* as in put, full
Long *ú* or *ů* as in ruler

Some consonants differ from English:

c is pronounced like ts in lots
č is like ch in cheap, chore
ch is like the Scottish loch or German Bach
ď sounds like dy (as some English speakers pronounce duty)
g is always like our g in gum, never like gem
j is like y in yes, never like joke or jam
ň sounds like ny as in canyon, or the Spanish pequeño
š is like sh in shoe
ť sounds like ty (as some English speakers pronounce tune)
ž is like z in seizure
ř has no equivalent in English. It is similar to the sound of rsh, but not quite. It must be learned by listening to a native speaker of Czech.